Dear Dave,

I thank you for your courage and your service and for your help in writing this bio.

My Brother Stevie: A Marine's Untold Story

Vietnam 1967

Mari and Stevie 1951

By

Marianne Kelsey Orestis

authorHOUSE®

AuthorHouse™ LLC
1663 Liberty Drive
Bloomington, IN 47403
www.authorhouse.com
Phone: 1-800-839-8640

Published by AuthorHouse 08/01/2014

ISBN: 978-1-4969-3048-4 (sc)
ISBN: 978-1-4969-3047-7 (e)

Library of Congress Control Number: 2014913491

Table of Contents

Preface

On June 2, 1967, I was one and a half years old. Today, I am 48 and a half years old. 47 years have ticked away since that day my Uncle Straughan (Stevie) died heroically on the field of battle. What have we missed and what did he miss? He was destined for leadership and greatness, and went to war to fight for what he believed was right. He was a leader from the day he arrived. The men he encountered remember him vividly to this day. The world lost a man that would have gone on to achieve great things in business and politics. A future CEO? Senator? Presidential candidate? As for him and so many others killed in Vietnam, we will never know.

In 1993, I moved to Washington, DC to begin the journey to my own future. I reached out to Stevie's boyhood friend and St. Paul's roommate, Senator John Kerry (who would go on to run for President of the United States and serve as Secretary of State). We had breakfast together one morning in the private Senate dining room. He told me stories about their adventures at school and backpacking together in Europe during the summer. He told me he had always admired Stevie and looked up to him as the one destined for great success and leadership. He told me he was crushed when he learned of his death, but knew he died a hero. He also told me the world lost a great man who would have made a great difference.

What have we missed and what did he miss? We missed a leader. We missed a hero. We missed a son, brother, uncle and husband. We missed greatness. Not a day has passed since he died that we don't feel his impact and his loss. This book tells the untold story of a Marine and a hero. And yet nothing will ever be able to tell the story of what we missed and of what he missed.

Christos Orestis III
July 4, 2014

Introduction

Lieutenant Straughan Downing Kelsey, Jr. was born to be a Marine. The first born of a career service officer and his military wife, Steve was born July 14, 1943 and gave his life for his country in Quang Tin Province, Republic of Vietnam on June 2-3, 1967. He is a hero and his story has never been told.

This book is dedicated to all the Marines of the
2nd Battalion 5th Marine Regiment
"F" Company 2nd Platoon.

Foxtrot 2nd Platoon
kneeling left – Captain Graham right – Lt Kelsey Jr

A Warrior Defined

The warrior stands for protecting loved ones and the highest ideals of civilization. The ideal warrior embodies virtue, strength, sacrifice, courage, discipline,and camaraderie. Most valued of the warrior is the protecting of what is most precious.

"Make no little plans; they have no magic to stir man's blood and probably themselves will not be realized. Make big plans; aim high in hope and work, remembering that a noble, logical diagram once recorded will not die." Saint Paul's School

"My legs you will chain; yes, but not my will; no, not even Zeus can conquer that." Epictetus

"Every man is frightened at first in battle; if he says he isn't, he is a god-damn liar. Some men are cowards, yes, but they will fight just the same, or get the hell scared out of them watching men who do fight; who are just as scared as they. The real hero is the man who fights even though he is scared. Some get over their fright in a few minutes even though he is scared. Some get over their fright in a few minutes in battle, some take hours, for some it takes days. The real man never lets the fear of death overpower his honor, his duty to his country, and his innate manhood." General George Patton in the speech to his Third Army preparing for invasion. England 5 July 1944

I still believe in God. I still believe in a good God. I believe He is like a Father, and that He loves us, wants the best for us, and hurts when we shun Him and His way. I believe we will never achieve what we long for the most apart from Him." Dr. Donald F. Wildmon

"Be strong and of good courage; fear not, nor be afraid of them; for the Lord thy God, He it is that doth go with thee: He will not fail thee, nor forsake thee." Deuteronomy 31:6

"Now see from this how vain it is to worry about things. It is all chance or destiny and our wayward footsteps are best planted without too much calculation. One must yield oneself simply and naturally to the mood of the game and trust in God which is another way of saying the same thing." Winston Churchill, England, 1940

"There is always a vague sense that every new trial has a meaning, that it was intended for me and that it will make me more pure, more worthy in respect of my conscience and, probably, in the eyes of God." Helene Berr, 1942. Written while a Jewess living in occupied France. In 1944 she was arrested and found stomped to death in the work camp the Nazis had sent her to.

"Now there's another thing I want you to remember. I do not want to get any message saying that we're holding our position. We're not holding anything. Let the Hun do that. We are advancing constantly and we're not interested in holding onto anything except the enemy. We're going to kick him in the ass. We're going to kick the hell out of him all the time and we're going to go through him like shit through a goose!" General George Patton

"I come in peace, I didn't bring artillery. But, I am pleading with you with tears in my eyes: if you fuck with me, I'll kill you all. Marine Corps General Mattis to Iraqi leaders.

"The strongest of all warriors are these two – Time and Patience." *War And Peace* by Leo Tolstoy

Mr. Louie Zamperini who participated in the 1930's Berlin Olympics and angered Hitler, placed as a track and field star for America, became an United States Air Force aviator and was shot down over the Pacific during WWII only to fight with sharks before being captured/rescued by the Japanese and as a POW beaten daily until the end of the War when he resumed a normal life.

The American's Creed

I believe in the United States of America, as a government
of the people, by the people, for the people:
Whose just powers are derived from the consent of the governed:
a democracy in a republic: a sovereign nation of many sovereign
states; a perfect union, one and inseparable: established upon
those principles of freedom, equality, justice and humanity for
which American patriots sacrificed their lives and fortunes.
I therefore believe it is my duty to my country to love it;
to support its constitution, to obey its laws, to respect
its flag, and to defend it against all enemies.

The American's Creed, by William Tyler Page was adopted by an act of Congress, April 6, 1918.

1943-1949

Straughan Downing Kelsey, Jr. was born July 14, 1943, at 5:35PM. He was born at Norwegian Hospital in Brooklyn, New York. The attending doctor was Bertram J. David. The first born of Captain Straughan Downing and Eileen Elizabeth Fee Kelsey weighed 7 pounds-15 ounces. He was 19 ½ " long and his eyes were blue. His complexion was fair and he had very little hair on top of his head but long and full at the nape of the neck. He was beautiful.

His father's name was Straughan Downing Kelsey, better known as Jack. Jack's parents were Doctor Harry Ray Kelsey and Novella Bart Downing Kelsey. His mother's name was Eileen Elizabeth Fee, better known as Bumpy. Her parent's names were John Michael Fee and Marguerite Tracy Fee.

Straughan Downing Kelsey, Jr.'s, known as Stevie by his family, first home was at 190 95th Street, Brooklyn, New York. The home was located in Brooklyn Heights, New York and was an historic brownstone near the park on the Hudson River.

Among the first gifts given to Stevie were a baby carriage, given by his Grandfather and Grandmother Kelsey, a bassinet and christening dress and slip given by his Grandma and Grandpa Fee; a christening coat and hat in blue silk, given by Aunt Marj Fee Waller; a silver cup, given by Uncle Bill Waller, a $100.00 war bond and a handmade suit, given by Uncle Gene and Aunt Myrtle Kelsey; a silver cup given by Aunt Katherine Kelsey; gifts given by the 323rd Bomb Squadron and various gifts given by friends of all the families. Daddy, Jack Kelsey, was off to war and not there for the birth or first year. Jack knew about the birth from a telegram sent by Marguerite Fee, his mother-in-law and he sent one to his wife, Bumpy that said,

Well done, sweetheart. I am proud of you. All my most magnanimous love to our general and to his wonderful mother. The whole bomb squadron is tickled pink. I love you.

Upon the celebration of Stevie's first month his father, Jack, sent him a letter dated August 14, 1943:

Dear Son,

Now that you re growing up, it's time we had a little man-to-man talk, so grid up your diapers and settle down for a session with your pop. A month might not seem very much to you, but on the anniversary of your first month of existence, I think it high time for you to learn several facts which until now you have been too young to understand. We'll begin with the fact that you were born in the camp of the Lord, because it's a cinch that without His help in giving your mother good solid sense and in guiding her, you would have gone the way of many another little war baby who was never born. But, God watched over you and your dear mother with great care, and because even when you were just a hope and a prayer, she was very cautious about what she did with you; along you came to life to bring a very great happiness to us.

Don't think, tho', that life is going to be all play for you! Far from it!! Now that you are the man of the family, you have a big job to do, and a delicate one. Your job is to take care of our beloved Bumpy, but you mustn't overdo it. So you go ahead and work conscientiously to keep Mother busy — kick your covers off, throw your toys away, pee in your little pants, do all sorts of things to make her work — but keep a good eye on her; if she looks tired, be sure to stop — go to sleep or something. And above all, don't be a nuisance at night. She worked hard making you and deserves lots of rest, so you be good when she sleeps! Just keep her busy, tho'— that's the secret of happiness for these women — as long as some man makes them work like a Trojan for him, they're happy as larks! That's the way I got your mother, bless her sweet heart, by treating her rough. She's a sweet thing, that beautiful mother of yours — mighty sweet. You will be damn lucky to do as well as I!!

While speaking of her, let me advise you to keep a civil tongue in yer head when ye speak to her or, bygorra, that Irish temper of hers will blow your head off. If you don't believe me, just go ahead and be a smart aleck. You'll learn!! But, bygorra, I love her for that temper and hope you have one just like it — a temper 'that knows no compromise when truth and right are in jeopardy'.

Well, son, your ol' daddy worked all yesterday, slept and worked in fits all last nite, worked all today, and must work tonight all nite, so he's going to stop now. Happy birthday, big boy!! You lucky stiff, how I'd like to swap places with you for a while. Give her a bite for me next time you see her, if you know what I mean. (Wink, wink!) And tell her I say 'Goodnite, sweetheart'.

Love and kisses, Father!! Captain S.D. Kelsey

When Stevie was six months old his father wrote him again. This letter is dated January 15, 1944:

Yesterday you were six months old! I can't believe it, it is impossible that you, my son, should be six whole months old when only yesterday you were only a fertile and fervent hope. And sitting up in a high chair already, too. Frankly, it dumbfounds me. Steve boy, you can't imagine how much I'd like to be there to congratulate you on your new tricks as you learn them, but we still have to beat these people so you can grow up tall and straight — physically, mentally and morally. It's quite a job and will take several months yet, but no matter what, you are going to have a free atmosphere in which to grow up to be the good soldier your daddy wishes he could be. Your mother has told me all about you and while it sure is nice to know how healthy you are and how quickly you are developing, it makes me homesick as (not for your tender ears — such words) to realize how much of you I am missing — not to see your bright little eyes or well-formed ears and head and your sleek little body. If only I could see you sitting in your high chair or watch for your first tooth or help you eat your chow! Someday you'll know, because your son will be born in the next war, but until then, believe me I sure do miss you. But before you develop a typically Kelsey conceit, let's stop talking of you.

As man-to-man, son, what do you think of our Little Precious (Little Precious, ma'am to you)? Have you ever known a better mother? Of course not. It ain't every young fellow who is so lucky as to have as smart and conscientious a mother as you have, to say nothing of her looks. Isn't she a honey, tho'? Just as pert as a new penny. And as sweet and nice as can be. Steve, you're going to grow up in a rough world, but if you ever do <u>anything</u> to hurt your mother, I forgive you for it but I shall never forget it. With your mother's qualities in you, I know you will never hurt her, tho'.

I have a treat for her, but don't tell her. It's a calendar with a picture of my "country retreat" on it. A good one, too. Ah, that's a wonderful place — I've just come back from 24 hours there. Gosh, but I hate to leave it. You know, Robbie (the manager) is just as proud of you two as I am. I doubt very much if anyone yet has spent a nite in the bar while I was there without seeing all my snapshots of you-all.

Well son it's pretty late now so I'll stop. Just wanted to tell you how much I miss you and to congratulate you on your half birthday. Please tell your mother that I love her and am lonely for her. Kiss her a couple of kisses for me.

Goodnite Steve, doggone your sweet little hide — I miss (--) out of you

Love and Kisses, Father Captain S.D. Kelsey

When Stevie was 11 months old he took his first car trip and it was a long one. Bumpy and Stevie drove from Brooklyn to Jack's hometown of Newport News, Virginia alone as Jack was off to war. It was a long and harrowing drive as Bumpy was not used to driving and had never left New York before. It was a short stay, however, and the next time they went to Newport News they went by train when Stevie was 13 months old.

At 11 months old Stevie weighed 21 pounds and was 29" long; he gained a full pound the next month. Stevie got his first tooth on April 3, 1944. He took his first step at 14 months. His first words were Da - Da, Ma - Ma, Chicki and Woo -Woo (dog). His favorite toys were an elephant, a saucepan and a spoon, a monkey named Heathcliff, and a telephone. Not much has changed in the lives of babies since.

He received mostly clothing for his first birthday along with a pair of white kid gloves. It was an adult party with relatives. By the time he reached his 3rd birthday he was talking very plainly, had a serious nature, had very intelligent eyes and also had many colds during the winter months. He had moved from Brooklyn to West Point, New York. And he had a sister, Marianne.

Stevie started nursery school when he was 4 years old. He contacted chicken pox in January of 1948 but his health, overall, was good. He had a slim build but was not skinny. He had a small frame all his life. When he turned 5 years old he went to kindergarten, at West Point. In kindergarten his health was good and he was resistant to colds except for a dry cough. Bumpy described him as very hard to handle, augmentative and stubborn, but, she went on to say that he was a good kid and loved his sister. She continued to say that he was polite and nice away from home and that he was very smart. He would later test out to an I.Q. of 160. He was becoming a real boy's boy, preferring boys' company, football, tanks and toy soldiers, electric trains, Roy Rogers and the Lone Ranger.

Stevie did a lot of moving around in his early years. His travels prepared him for the military life and the moving that goes with it. When he was 11 months old he traveled to Newport News, Virginia and back to Brooklyn. When he was 14 months old he made the trip again. At age 2 he made the first of many trips to Wethersfield, Connecticut (where Bumpy's family was); this time with his baby sister, Marianne.

In March of 1946 Daddy came home from war. The young family moved to Brookline, Massachusetts. In July of 1946, at age 3, the family moved to West Point Military Academy where his father became an instructor. There were many trips to Connecticut and Brooklyn to visit family. Shortly after that event the family moved again; this time to Clovis Field in Albuquerque, New Mexico.

I remember five things about that stay: Stevie went to the state fair and won the penny toss and for his efforts he won a baby chick. We put the baby chick in the furnace room to keep it warm but it died anyway. Stevie was devastated. He was always a sensitive person. We visited an Indian Reservation and along the way gave a ride to three Indian children who were walking up the hill to their home. My mother put a sheet over the back seat of the car in case they had germs. It was an offense. When we got to the Reservation my father took pictures of their land and home and holy sites. The Indian Chief came over and grabbed the camera out of Daddy's hands and took the film out, as the Chief was fearful we had captured their spirit world.

We had a garden in the backyard and we grew a carrot so large and big in circumference that it took the strength of Daddy, Stevie and myself to pull it out of the ground. We were introduced to horseback riding during this stay and it is a love that endured. I went picking flowers at school during recess. The only problem was the flowers were on the cactus and I got needles all over my hands. The school nurse was very upset and wrapped my hands in bandages to pull the needles out.

1950-1958

In 1950, the family was transferred to Montgomery, Alabama, where Maxwell Field Air Force Military Base was. At Montgomery, Stevie went to Camp Grist, a summer camp, located in Selma which would ten years later become the scene of the famous civil rights march on Selma. He then started attending first grade at the military base's school. He also received his First Communion. Stevie and I shared a bedroom with bunk beds. At Halloween we went Treat or Treating and came back to the house with lots of candy. I dumped mine in the middle of the bedroom floor and started eating it all. Stevie, very methodically took out his candy and separated it into sections and types of candy. He then only ate a small part of the stash and saved the rest for later nights. This was typical of Stevie, always thinking ahead and very precise in his thinking. His father was promoted to Lt. Colonel and then to Colonel, becoming the youngest serviceman to be so honored and promoted. In 1952, Stevie's sister, Lisa Bart, was born at Montgomery, Alabama. Then we were stationed to Korea.

The family got all their immunizations for the trip, but the Korean War intensified and Daddy was ordered to command Taegu Air Base in Southern Korea so we could not go with him. My mother chose to move the family to Florida to wait out the war. My father saw us settled into our new home in Lake Worth, Florida and he left for two tours of duty in Korea.

We were a pioneering family in Lake Worth. The city was just being developed and we lived in a newly built two-bedroom home on the edge of the settlement; there was no air conditioning Now it is located in the middle of town. My mother planted two Royal Palm trees in the front yard and they grew to be very tall. They eventually died and the new owners of the house planted two new ones. We lived in Lake Worth for two years. We spent part of the summers at Lake Tahoe Motel and it had a pool and there was a diner nearby that sold foot long hot dogs with ketchup, relish and mustard that we all ate and they were very good. We went with a group of mother's friends and children and stayed at the motel for two weeks. It was an adventure and a lot of fun with swimming being the order of the day.

The beach was right next to the motel and we went there and played in the waves. Stevie was not very adventurous, but he enjoyed it even so. His sister, Lisa Bart reports that she fell into the pool at the motel and sunk to the bottom of the pool when she saw a white light and a hand come out of the depths of the pool and it was Stevie who grabbed and pulled her to safety. She was eighteen months old. He was the protector of the family from day one for both my sister and myself and my mother. He took his responsibility as first born extremely seriously.

We attended a catholic school and Stevie attended mass every day and was an altar boy. We had no television, but the people next door did so in the late afternoon Stevie and I would go to their house to watch Howdy Doody. We looked forward to this daily ritual with great excitement. We also played Mumbly Peg, a game played with a knife. We would throw the knife into the sand to see if it would stick up straight. It was a lot of fun. Stevie was adept at rifle practice, his aim was exceptional. Mother and the two of us would also try and grow grass for a lawn, but all we got were weeds, especially the pesky, troublesome and hurtful sand spurs. The relatives started moving into the area also at this time.

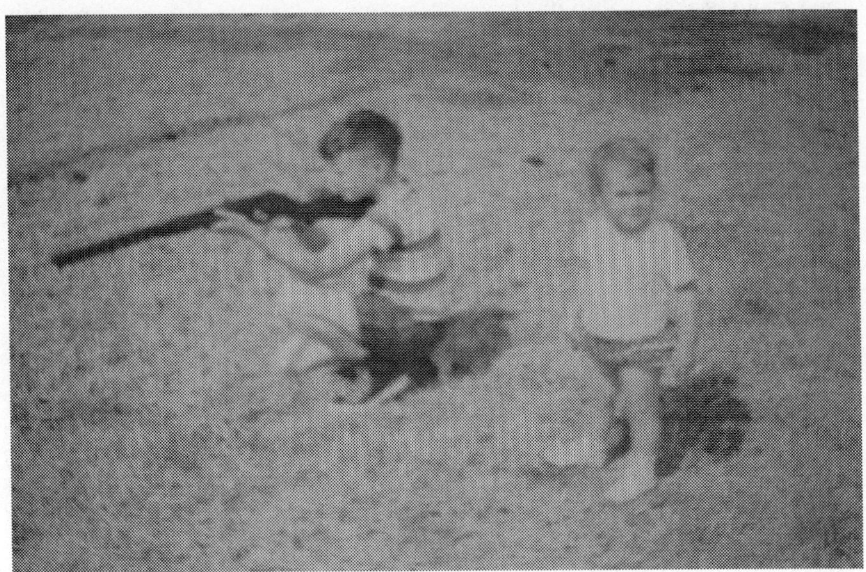

Rifle practice in Florida in 1951

First came Grandpa and Grandma Fee. They bought a new house in Lake Worth and moved, lock stock and barrel from Brooklyn. They retired in Lake Worth and loved their property. It was all pink, inside and out; Grandma's favorite color. The house was so newly built it didn't have a lawn for a long time. There was no pool with the house, but it had an outside patio which was not screened in. It was all very nice and my mother loved having them so close by. Also to come and stay was Grandfather Kelsey, who was affectionately called Kels. He arrived with his new wife, a genteel Southern Belle, called Irene. His first wife, Novella Bart Kelsey, had died in 1943 of cancer. They came fromVirginia and settled in as well. My mother had built up quite a community of friends and family and school and church when Father came home from war in 1954. Lisa was two years old, I was eight years old and Stevie was 10 years old.

It was a very exciting time. Stevie and I were at school when the principal called us out of our respective classrooms and we went to the office to see my mother there with Lisa. She said, "Come with me to the airport, your Father is home." So we went to Boca Raton Air Field, which is now Florida Atlantic University, and got there just as Daddy was getting off the plane. He was larger than life and was wearing his flight suit and his Air Corps hat with the Colonel's insignia on it. He was carrying a very large Korean bow with a sling of arrows over his arm. He had a huge smile and enveloped all of us in his arms. He took charge right away and whisked us home to a wonderful homecoming celebration.

He bought a lawn mower and cut the weeds in the yard and suddenly we had a lawn. He met Mother's friends and their families and he met Irene, who was eight years older than him. They hit it off right away and everything was just fine, but he had news.

We were transferred to Washington D.C. where my Father was to report for duty at the Pentagon. So, sadly, we packed up, rented the house out to strangers, got in the Buick and drove to Falls Church, Virginia, where we settled into an older house in a development called Sleepy Hollow. Stevie and I were enrolled in a catholic school, called Saint Anthony's. It was a new school and church as that whole area of suburban Virginia was in the process of a development explosion. What was farmland when we first arrived became four lane highways and shopping centers just three years later.

Stevie thrived at school. At that phase in his life he was medium height, with short, curly hair inherited from his Grandma Fee. He was pale and a bit of a recluse who preferred reading books and building model planes to playing outside. He was an extremely handsome young man with an engaging smile that lit up his whole face and his eyes. He served as a School Safety Patrol for two years. He got to keep the cherished patrol belt on while riding in the school bus to and from school, keeping order on the bus. He held great respect amongst his peers and kept order with no problem at all. He was also a First Class Boy Scout. One night in Falls Church Lisa came into Stevie's bedroom and knelt at his bed and asked him if he would marry her when she got older. His reply was quite compassionate and he told her he could not marry her because he was her brother but when he got older he would look for a woman that had the qualities of Lisa because he loved her very much and felt protective of her.

His genius began to blossom in Falls Church. He was always on the honor roll and was an example for other students. He began piano lessons at the age of 10 years. The lessons started because Mother wanted to learn to play and Stevie showed an interest in her lessons. So she said to him, "If you can learn to play this piece, I will quit lessons and give them to you." He did learn and went on to become a brilliant pianist and later guitarist who played slide guitar once with Bo Diddley. His passion for music was born and he entered recitals and introduced me to Joan Baez, Bob Dylan, Beachboys and the Kingston Trio when they were just starting out. The music that he played was varied, from pop to classical. Some of the pieces were for the organ as well. He practiced scales and chords; he played sentimental and old time music. He played Broadway tunes for guitar, organ, and piano. Stevie played songs written by the difficult composer Irving Berlin. And finally, he was introduced to the Beatles and played their music and played it magnificently. At this same time, he also took art lessons and was a gifted artist, drawing way beyond his young years. Only a few paintings remain and they are irreplaceable. It was also at this period in our lives that we added a new member to the family: Brandy of K- Bac or, as he was better known, Pierre. Pierre was a chocolate royal grand standard poodle and he was a beauty to behold. He was always dignified, extremely intelligent, and learned his lessons well. He lived with the family in all our moves and died at the age of 21.

We continued to live in Falls Church until 1955 and moved to a newer development in Lake Barcroft. It was located within the Virginia –Washington D.C. suburbs. Lake Barcroft was definitely upscale from what we were used to living in. The house had three floors and four bedrooms. It had a dining room, a living room, and a finished basement. The house was built of white brick with a pink front door. There was a carport attached. The yard was very large and fenced in with a picket fence for Pierre.

There was a forest surrounding the side and back of the house. There were lots of military families living in this area and all of the fathers worked at the Pentagon. There was a large man made lake, hence the name Lake Barcroft. In the summer there were always swimming races and activities at the lake. It was a very cohesive community. It was during this time that Stevie and I appeared on a Washington, DC television station's show, "The Milt Grant Record Hop." The show was a precursor of the "American Bandstand" which originated out of Pennsylvania. We appeared on the "Milt Grant Record Hop" twice and the last time we were on the show Johnny Mathis appeared and sang a song on the live television show. He was just starting out and was very popular. After the show was over, we went to the elevator and so did Johnny Mathis and we rode in the elevator together, just the three of us. This occurrence was extremely unusual as security for the stars was elevated because Bobby Darin had been on the show a few days before and his clothes had gotten torn by fans in the elevator. I went to the far corner of the elevator and whispered to Stevie to ask for his autograph but Stevie, shy as he was refused. I'm sure Johnny Mathis could hear our whole conversation and was quite amused by us. Stevie made sure we were on the camera most of the time. He was my dancing partner. We got a lot of exposure on the Record Hop and it was a lot of fun. Stars like Ella Fitzgerald, Frankie Lane, Crash Craddock, Annette Funicello, Frankie Avalon, Brenda Lee, Dean Hawley and others were featured artists on the show. We had both learned how to do the jitterbug and the waltz at ballroom dancing school in Virginia.

Stevie and I continued attending Saint Anthony's school, but in the year 1956-1957 I switched to a public school, Bailey's Crossroads' Elementary, and Stevie prepared to graduate from the 8th grade. Due to his genius, he applied for and won a scholarship to Saint Paul's Preparatory School in Concord, New Hampshire, a most prestigious boarding school. I remember traveling by car to New Hampshire to see the school.

Stevie as he entered Saint Paul's in the summer of 1957

We had traded in the old, worn out Buick with a brand new Chevrolet pink station wagon, complete with the then fashionable tailfins. Stevie was all packed up with trunks and suitcases and the car was full. We went in early Fall and traveled country roads. The ride was beautiful, as New England, in the Fall, can be. The school was located no more than 1 ½ hours from Cheshire, Connecticut, where Aunt Marj, Mother's sister, lived with her family of three young boys; Jack, Bob and Steve Waller and her husband Bill.

Aunt Marj's home would come to be a home away from home for Stevie; she became a surrogate mother to him. His cousins were like his own brothers. In the nearby area of Cheshire there was more family for Stevie as Great Aunt Carrie, Marguerite Fee's sister, lived with her husband, Fred Sehl; their children had grown and stayed in the area.

In September of 1957, Stevie wrote a letter home from his first month at school. The letter was written in good spirits and Stevie was having fun and learning a lot. His French teacher spoke only French during class and his Latin teacher was an old fat man with a crew cut. His English teacher was an Englishman who assigned them books of "Mythology" and "A Book of Short Stories" rather than grammar exercises. For Sacred Studies he studied out of a book called "The History of the Hebrew Commonwealth" and the "Old Testament." He took Algebra and liked his teacher. He was doing well in Math and not finding it too difficult. Math would remain one of his best subjects. For someone who had been a bookworm all his short life of 13 years, he jumped into school sports activities and joined the football team. He was assigned the fifth team where he was a tackle. His club was called the "Old Hundreds."

The students did calisthenics everyday and Stevie was getting sore. There was a swimming test which Stevie passed with ease. To entertain the boys, the faculty showed movies and the first one was *Doctor At Sea* along with a Bugs Bunny cartoon which Stevie enjoyed. Classes started at at 8:35AM and went until 1:00PM with a break for lunch at 1PM. Classes resumed at 2:30PM and went until 5:35PM. There was a study hall from 7:45-8:45PM. A letter from school indicated that Stevie's Group Master would be Mr. David W. Waters and his responsibilities were to be a friend to Stevie and a conduit of support and information to his parents.

The second letter home described the first football game in which Stevie made a wonderful tackle from behind the fellow carrying the ball. It was great for a bookworm who was skinny at that. He also described how he wanted to play LaCrosse, a game he ended up playing for 8 years. He met his best friend, Bill Kean, and they enjoyed a paper wad game or spit wad with the wads flying all over the dorm. Mr. Waters had to intervene and Stevie said he would quiet down from then on. He had a visit from Aunt Carrie and Uncle Fred who took him out to dinner and he enjoyed that very much.

He wrote home but this time with requests: his B-58 bomber airplane was broken and he needed special glue to repair it. The weather turned cold so he needed extra blankets or a comforter. He wanted a West Point flag and flags and medals and emblems from the services with which to decorate his room. He needed a hunting knife and his "Air Force Survivor Manual." And, most of all, he wanted a camera with a flash. He was doing well.

On October 20, 1957, Stevie wrote that he had just finished up his first fortnight exams and would pass on his grades as soon as he got them. He said his "head was swimming" from the task. Saint Paul's played their first football game and won, Stevie was very proud. The school had several Roman Catholic students and the school took them to Sunday Mass at Saint Paul's, a church in Concord. Saint Paul's School was Episcopal. Stevie described it as very modern but the priests were very old and droll. He didn't like it. This resulted in attempts to find an alternate to this church, but, in the end, the school failed to find one. Stevie got into the school services, which were daily and very joyous. On trips into town, Stevie had a much needed hamburger and milkshake and bought a goldfish, seaweed and a bowl. In this letter he wrote out the numbers, in French, 1-20. He had never spoken French before or been exposed to the language.

By October 27th his grades were in and they were as follows: Sacred Studies-86, English-70, Latin-88, French-92, Algebra-85 for an average on the Blue List of 84.2, placing him ninth in the class. In a letter dated the same day he talks about the 35,000 volume library on campus and the books on aviation and science fiction. He talks about his piano studies and how, in his mind, they are not going well. In a letter to the school his father talked about his piano playing and how he had to study very hard to master a piece of classical yet learned pop very easily and seemed to love it best. For Christmas he desired ice skates and wanted to see if a Mr. Alan's ski's would fit him. For a boy who stayed indoors all the time and read and worked on models he was throwing himself into sports and seeming to love it. The letter went on to say that he had joined the Rifle club at school and had learned to shoot in a prone position and would learn kneeling and standing positions soon. He wrote about walking through the New Hampshire woods and liking the New England woodland better than the southern woods.

In November he thanked the family for sending him a comforter, a parka, and flashlight batteries. He also sent a thank you note to Aunt Carrie and Uncle Fred Sehl for taking him out to dinner again and invited them to come visit him during the day when he could give them a tour of the school. He talked about his time crunch in getting everything required of him done, from studies to piano to sports to eating. Exams were coming up and he wasn't sure he would have time to study for them. His French was taking a nosedive in grades because he was put in a higher class, but he said he was beginning to catch on and doing better, so not to worry.

He sent home two compositions, one from English class and one from French class. Remembering that Stevie did not speak a word of French only three months prior to this paper, he wrote a two page story about his house, all in French, and he got an 86 on it. The title of the paper was "La Maison de Steve Kelsey." It flowed with descriptions of his home in Virginia, the colors, and the different floors, and what each individual room was used for. He wrote for two pages, both sides of the papers, and made very few mistakes. It was entirely in French with all the spelling and grammar correct and proper. In his senior year he would go on to win the the school's French speaking and writing prize: a set of red, leather-bound books all in French. The books were beautiful and he was very proud of them. They now rest in the Saint Paul's library.

The English composition was science fiction, telling the tale of a 23rd century writer describing World War III which took place in 1960 and destroyed the world political scene. He was graded a C+ but the story was very telling of times to come in our own 21st century. The story describes how the Russians, during the Cold War, infiltrating different countries with spies and terrorists to prepare them for the big day, December 25, 1960 when they would come out from undercover and take over the free world by planting tanks loaded with thermonuclear bombs, in the middle of major cities in America and bombing the cities.

At the same time the Russians would have converted many countries, such as China, Korea, Japan, Egypt, Syria, Jordan, Libya and Iraq, to join them in a great world coup. The next day, December 26, 1960, most of North and South America, England, Russia, Europe, Asia and the northern part of Africa were nothing but crater filled land masses burning with radiation. Those in the 23rd century had been trying to remove the deadly effects of the radiation but were being unsuccessful and decided that the only thing left to do was to evacuate to Mars. He anticipated the future of 2001 and beyond.

Stevie started off December 1, 1957, by writing to the family about his Thanksgiving holiday and meal, all of which happened at the school. Each table of students had at its head a 20 pound turkey with all the trimmings. Some of the older students volunteered to dress up as waiters and serve the meal which Stevie described as "lavish." After the dinner feast the students went ice skating on one of the larger ponds. The letter concludes with his Christmas wish list which was modest to say the least. It included a wish for a flash camera that would take color slides, some models, money and a canteen. The letter of December 7, 1957 tells of checks arriving from the Fee's and, once more, asking for hockey gear, including ice skates and gloves for skating. He said exams were coming up and all he had to do the week before the exams was to rest and study so that was good for him as he had been worried about having enough time to do everything. He was a perfectionist.

Just prior to the exams he had to write an essay on love and the Shakespearean quote, "It is better to have loved and lost than not to have loved at all." His first sentence of the essay was "Bah! How foolishly romantic can you get?" The essay describes a soap opera telling of a jilted love and how it turns out all right. He went on with his essay to give a real life scenario where it would still turn out all right. The essay and his thoughts belie his life wherein he had one true love, Donna S., who he dated during his years at Saint Paul's and Princeton and married January 7, 1967. Stevie was truly a romantic.

On December 17, 1957, the grades came out and a report from Mr. David Waters was included. Mr. Waters reported that Stevie had a good first term but that his grades had dropped off a bit during the second quarter. Mr. Waters was not worried about this and said his grades would improve over time. He described Stevie as quiet but sociable and that he was perfectly at ease with the other boys. He wished all a Merry Christmas and Happy New Year and signed off. Stevie's grades were included and they went as follows: Sacred Studies-83, English-79, Latin-85, French-81, Algebra-88 for an average of 83.2 and a ranking of 15th in a class of 89.

Then he traveled by train to Washington, D.C. for the holiday. It would be the last holiday at 6725 Joallen Drive, Falls Church, Virginia, as we were to be getting new travel orders.

When Steve returned to school he had traveled in style, flying Military Air Transport System to New Hampshire. He described the flight as follows: "After we took off from Washington the hostess served breakfast. We had French toast, ham, tea and grapefruit. Then we landed in Philadelphia and after a short stay there we took off for Boston. On the way I had a cup of coca. Then we got to Boston and had to wait an hour for another plane. When we finally arrived in Concord I got a taxi from the school and then ate lunch. After that I went ice skating all afternoon."

The next day they got two feet of snow and it got down to minus 9. His fish bowl, which he had bought earlier in the season, froze, but it was a fake fish, so no harm done. In English class, the teacher sang the song "Frankie and Johnnie" and had the class in hysterics as he was so comical and fat, his other studies were doing well.

In his letter of January 26, 1958, he complained about the weather being so changeable as New England weather can be; first it snows and gets cold, then it warms up and rains and ruins the ice for skating. He reported that his ice skating and hockey skills were getting along pretty well and that he had a great lift. There had been no sleighing although there was plenty of snow but it had begun to rain. He was using his new camera quite a bit getting shots of the school and a jam session he came upon one night. He was taking Manuel Arts and had just finished an ice boat he had been working on prior to the holiday and now he was starting a voodoo mask that he described as "looking hideously swell." He also commented on his new squirt gun that worked so well and helped him to win battles. For entertainment the school showed two new films, "Silk Stockings" and "Richard the III", which he said was really weird.

On February 8, 1958 Stevie wrote that there was enough snow on the ground that it was up to the knees. His father, the Colonel, also told him that we were being transferred to Paris, France; the first besides my father to know. Stevie was very excited as was Dad. Stevie and Dad were the only ones who spoke any French and Stevie was rather proud of that fact.

He went on to write about The Mish, which is short for Missionary Society and it was a great fair which was a great fun. The school raffled off a 1958 Vespa motor scooter won by the grounds keeper. The school also brought in the Yale Bull Pups and a singer from National Records called Chip Fischer. Chip sang songs like the "Rock Island Line" and the Bull Pups played Dixieland and jazz for the students. There were booths and other things that carnivals have and it was a great time.

February 15th he finished the voodoo mask and said it was really hideous with feathers and horns and fangs and other things on it. He played an ice hockey game against another Saint Paul's team and lost but his spirits were up. Saint Paul's varsity team played against Andover and beat them 5-0, "it was quite a game". His dorm got a new superintendent and he was stricter than the former super, confiscating squirt guns and deodorant bottles The boys in the dorm also fought with water balloons.

Stevie reported that he had started going to the dentist, Doctor Miller, who just tightened the braces on his teeth. On the 23rd another letter was written and it reported more snow had fallen and that he had been in the infirmary for three days with a bad cough. He had a lot of fun there so he was not too sick. He played cards and other games. In his French class the students were reading "The Count of Monte Cristo" and his grades were up. His hockey team finally won a game and that was thrilling for him but it was awfully cold and he nearly froze to death.

On February 11th the Rector wrote to Dad that they could not make an exemption of Stevie leaving school before the end of the school year, June 13th. Dad was trying to have the whole family travel together to France; he would later be successful in getting the Air Force to postpone his departure date, which was exceptional, and we ended up all traveling together.

March 9, 1958, Stevie wrote that he saw another play, this time put on by the Sixth Form, about Saint Paul's going co-ed. Stevie said the play was very funny and scary. Saint Paul's did go co-ed eventually and it would work out fine. Stevie was preparing for his mid-term break and said he would like to visit friends and relatives. He was very close with his cousins and grandparents. He stated that he would like to take crew and that he already had started preparations by going to the first practice and doing calisthenics. He also ran a mile and thought the whole adventure would be a lot of fun.

The next Saturday his Form was putting on the play "Richard III" and they were doing some heavy advertising for it and thought it would go over well as it was so funny. He ended his letter by writing that he had lost his wristwatch in a wrestling match sponsored by the school. He lost the match.

On March 15th the school sent a letter home saying that Stevie had an aptitude for languages and suggested that he take up the study of Greek. The letter went on to say that if he chose to study Greek it would help him immensely but would cut into his choice of electives in the higher forms at the school. Stevie opted to study Greek. In his Sacred Studies he studied Isaiah and wrote an excellent paper on Isaiah called "Isaiah: Patriot and Prophet." In the paper he started with Isaiah's word's, "Here I am! Send me!" He went on to write his premise: "With these words Isaiah gave up his whole life in order to speak the word of Jehovah to Judah and save the country from destruction." He wrote for three pages about vice and corruption and about the bad King Hezekiah and got an 82. The paper was very thoughtful and accurate and showed his learning and insight and comprehension of what he was studying.

In April there were letters back and forth about Stevie's curriculum and between the school and our parents. It was decided that Stevie would take the following courses:

Fourth Form — English, Latin, Algebra, French, European History

Fifth Form — English, Geometry, Sacred Studies, Greek, Chemistry

Sixth Form — English, Mathematics, Greek, American History, Physics
He would continue piano but study pop music instead of classical. Quite possibly he would enter the Debate Team.

April 13th Stevie returned from vacation and in a letter requested his squirt guns and a machine gun that squirted water. He was still a little kid. The letter of April 27th stated that the buds were out on the trees The school council closed the "tuck shop" which was where the boys bought their candy and popsicles. It was closed due to littering in the area, but a Good Humor Man came around and the boys bought ice cream from him. The boys got one past the school council. He also said his grades were due and he would report as soon as he knew. Over that weekend he went spear-fishing and played tennis. His Form's play, "Richard III," was performed and went over very well.

Stevie's grades for the Third Form came in covering the period of March 6-May 3, 1958. For Sacred Studies he received an 82, for English he received an 81, for Latin he received an 88, for French he received an 84, for Algebra he received a 95 for an overall average of 86. Most wonderful.

On May 10th, Stevie wrote of fine weather and playing tennis and hiking. On his crew team, they sank the boat and the coach was a bit upset about it and the boys thought it all very funny. He mentioned the upcoming trip to France on the USS America (the luxury liner we would take to Paris, France) and said there were others from school who would be on the ship. In French class they were studying French monuments and cities, all in French, so he was prepared for the trip.

His final grades came in on June 15th and he was ranked 10th in his class of 88 pupils. The Group Masters report was very complimentary of Steve and his ability, considering Stevie to have a very solid academic achievement and thought he did well under pressure and that he would do well in his college boards in the future. For Sacred Studies he received a yearly average of 84, for English he received a yearly average of 84, for Latin he received a yearly average of 87, for French he received a yearly average of 83, for Algebra he received a yearly average of 93 with an overall average of 86.2 for the year. In the final letter of the school year Administrative Vice Rector William A. Oates wrote that Stevie had received another scholarship in the amount of $1,300.00 for the school year 1958-1959.

We were scheduled to travel to France on board the USS America. It would take five days to cross the Atlantic and we traveled in style. First, we stayed at Governor's Island in New York Harbor. Governors Island was a military outpost that was reserved for officers going overseas. We were treated very well. In June 1958 the five Kelsey's and Pierre sailed for France. We had separate staterooms. I stayed with two other girls who were older than I was and we got along fine. Pierre stayed in the kennel on the top deck and got walked every day by white coated servants and was fed filet mignon for dinner. I visited him every day. He was very happy. There were classmates of Stevie on board as well.

Saint Paul student John Kerry, SPS '62 was on board as well as two other students. There also were young people on board who were service children and on their way to France also. We all formed a group and played cards and went up on the deck at night to romance a bit. I was too young and thought it amusing. John Kerry was going to visit his grandmother in Brittany, France, where she had a chateau.

John and Stevie were to spend the summer together traveling by bicycle along the coast of France. They would repeat this trip each summer for three summers, until they graduated from Saint Paul's. Both spoke French fluently. John Kerry later went on to Yale University and then on to serve in the US Navy as a pilot and fight in Vietnam. Upon his return, he founded Vietnam Veterans against the War and was highly criticized for his role in trying to end the war. He later became a US Senator from Massachusetts and in 2004 ran for the Presidency of the United States. He was defeated by George Bush, the incumbent. His running mate was Senator John Edwards. He would become The Honorable Secretary of State serving under President Barack H. Obama.

Some years later Senator Kerry told me he was in politics because of the loss of life in the war and was trying to make sense of the deaths of so many heroes and potential leaders of the country. He most graciously had breakfast with my son Christos Orestis III in the Senate dining room and there were three chairs at the table: one for the Senator and one for Christos and one for Stevie. He was heavily involved with the Vietnam Memorial Building Committee.

Five days after leaving the United States of America we landed at Le Havre seaport and took a train to Paris. We stayed in a Chinese hotel on the

Champs Elysee. We stayed there about a week and took in the sights. The French were very taken with Pierre and called him the great poodle.

We left the hotel and moved into a house in Le Vesinet in the suburbs of Paris; it was a quick train ride from Paris. It was a lovely old-style French home with three floors and a Spanish maid, Maria. She made the best fried eggplant and was an excellent cook and house maid. My father bought a motorcycle for us to ride into town to go to the market or the boucherie. He tried to give us the French experience and we lived off base and did not associate with too many Americans. I rode the motorcycle also and burned the inside of my left calf on the engine and it produced a third degree burn which left a scar. Le Vesinet was very beautiful and there were parks and gardens all over.

We spent the summer adjusting to a new world and I can remember my father saying one day, "I am going into Paris today." He was very pleased with himself as he was in love with France. It was during the summer that we traveled to Belgium to see the World's Fair of 1958. It was grand and large and there was an awful lot to see and smell and taste. It was quite an experience. That ended our summer.

Stevie was to report back to New Hampshire, USA, to rejoin his class. He was a sophomore that year. We would not see him until the following summer. He spent his holidays with the Waller's: Aunt Marjorie, Uncle Bill, Jack, Bob and Steve. They lived in Cheshire, Connecticut. Lisa was enrolled in the SHAPE (Supreme Headquarters Allied Powers Europe) Village (a NATO school) first grade which taught in French only and I was enrolled in a private boarding school in Paris called Marymount which taught in French and English; I was in the 8th grade.

No letters or correspondence remains of Stevie's next three years at Saint Paul's, but I do know he loved the school and it became his spiritual home. He vacationed with the Waller's, Aunt Marj's family with three boys, Jack, Bob and Steve, that were in his age group. He spent a lot of time with the Sehl's who were Aunt Marj's Great Aunt Carrie and Uncle Fred; they were the sister and brother-in-law of Aunt Marj's and Mom's mother, Marguerite Tracy Fee.

In June of 1961 Straughan Downing Kelsey, Jr. graduated with honors from Saint Paul's School and not only had he learned academically, but spiritually as well, embodying the entire concept of the private church school that was Saint Paul's. Honor, truth, and trust were his foundation with his peers and elders and youngsters alike. He held the highest respect for all people and wanted to know as much as he could about others and their cultures and their languages and history and their spiritual beliefs. He was as honest as the day is long and not only with people but with government and property alike. He believed in the community of man and its collective highest calling. And that is why he finally joined the Marines. But, first there was Princeton University to attend.

Saint Paul's Class of 1961 Graduation photo

At Princeton University he majored in European History and languages, German in particular. He joined the Colonial Club, a Greek type school community organization. He boarded at the Club and was popular with his clubmates and classmates alike. He graduated in June of 1965 with a B average. He was held in the highest of esteem by his peers and family alike.

Upon his death this is what his friends from Princeton University wrote of him:

"Steve Kelsey was killed in action in South Vietnam in early June of this year. He had gone to Southeast Asia after completing the course in Vietnamese at the Defense Language Institute in Monterey, California, where he graduated first in his class. A Lieutenant in the Marine Corps, Steve was appointed platoon commander in a rifle company and led two small but successful clearing operations without taking any casualties. He was killed on the second day of a regimental 'search and destroy' campaign during which he was in the lead company. Only one of four officers in that unit survived the battle.

Steve was born on July 14, 1943 in Brooklyn, N.Y.. The son of an Air Force officer, his early years were spent on the move among various military posts around the country. Steve attended Saint Paul's School in Concord, New Hampshire. During those four years, his family was stationed with S.H.A.P.E. In Paris and he spent his summers traveling on the Continent, perfecting his French: he went on to win a first prize in French at Saint Paul's.

At Princeton, Steve was a member of Colonial Club, where he lived during his senior year. He wrote his thesis on eighteenth century German history and played junior varsity lacrosse. Those who knew Steve appreciated his soft-spoken manner, his wry sense of humor, and his cultivated charm. His attitude toward life was relaxed, but his values were as solid as a rock.

After graduation Steve seemed interested only in a career of government service, either with the State Department or the Marine Corps. While awaiting the beginning of O.C.S., he taught as a substitute teacher in the Florida school system, where he was he was highly regarded by principals and students alike. In the Marines, Steve finished the Officer's Basic Course third in his class, honor man in his platoon, company commander, first in military aptitude, and president of the Junior Officer's Dining-In.

At Princeton, Steve had met a Vassar girl named Donna who soon became a constant fixture around Colonial Club and a respected friend of Steve's college companions. Steve and Donna became engaged in November 1966 and were married on January 8, 1967, in Illinois, honeymooning at the Presidio of Monterey.

Steve once said, 'I do seem to have a certain aptitude for the Marines,' and in Vietnam he was impatient at the delay in being able to lead his men in combat. After the battle in which Steve was killed, the men of his unit wept openly at their loss. The Class of 1965 is proud to have known Steve and extends its sympathy and regrets to his wife and family.

On August 25th of 2012, a Memorial Service was held in his honor in the State of Maine. It was officiated by Congressman Michael Michaud, D-ME and Pastor Peter H. Stetson of First Apostolic Church. In attendance were members of his sister, Marianne's family, members of Rolling Thunder, a full military honor guard and readings by the Congressman and members of the Princeton class of 1965 herein included:

In Remembrance of Steve Kelsey

25 August 2012

As members of the Princeton Class of 1965 and fellow Marines we wish to express our best wishes, thoughts and prayers to the family and friends of our classmate, 2nd Lieutenant Straughan D. Kelsey, Jr. USMC, who gave his life for his country on June 3, 1967.

"Steve" as he was known to friends and family, was "the best of the best" of an otherwise distinguished Princeton class. He was a gentleman, a scholar and a patriot, admired by one and all. Following graduation, he volunteered to serve his country as an officer in the United States Marine Corps, choosing the most demanding of the military services as would be expected of Steve. He was satisfied only if he succeeded in the most challenging of circumstances.

Steve excelled at both Marine Corps Officer Candidate School and Infantry Basic School in Quantico, Virginia, finishing both rigorous programs at the top of his class of Marine officers. Steve was a true leader and it was in that capacity – as as leader of Marines – that he lost his life in Vietnam. It was reported that his men, all battle-tested Marines, wept at Steve's passing, a testament to the quality of his leadership and the compassion he held for those who were his responsibility.

Those of us who served in Vietnam and were fortunate to have returned have not forgotten Steve Kelsey or our other fallen Marine classmate, 1st Lieutenant David S. Hackett, or the more than 59,000 other American service personnel who lost their lives in Vietnam. It was in that spirit that a group of us banded together and financed the construction of the Kelsey-Hackett Kindergarten near Dong Ha, Quang Tri province, Vietnam, building a school in their names to provide early educational opportunities to young Vietnamese students.

Having been given the gift of continuing life, we have dedicated ourselves to lead our respective lives in a manner that would make Steve and Dave proud – proud to have been their classmates, and proud to have been given the honor to be called "Marines".

Steve will be in our thoughts on August 25, 2012 as he is every day.

Karl J. Ege '65	John W. Keker '65	Robert W. Norton '65
Captain USMC	1st Lieutenant USMC	Captain USMC

A strong sense of family and pride in the Air Force came through in his letters. He was very proud of the history of war and aviation that ran through the family and there was a sense that he wanted to share in it as he did when he joined the United States Marine Corps. He loved airplanes but when he grew old enough to take flying lessons he discovered that he became airsick and could not fly, hence his enlistment in the infantry. He served with honor and distinction and in his last battle lead with uncommon valor.

1958-1961

After the 1958-59 school year ended, Stevie came home to France. We had moved out of Le Vesinet to a S.H.A.P.E. community called SHAPE Village, located in Saint Germaine-en-Laye, also a suburb of Paris. S.H.A.P.E. was an acronym for Supreme Headquarters Allied Powers Europe and has since relocated to Brussels, Belgium. Daddy had a very high level position there and I think he was second in command. Stevie joined us along with our grandparents, the Fee's. Together we saw all the sights of Paris and spent Stevie's favorite day of the year, July 14th-Bastille Day in Paris in an apartment overlooking the Place de la Concorde. We watched the incredible fireworks and listened to the beautiful music celebrating France's Independence and, so Stevie thought, his day. We visited the surrounding communities, including Fontainebleau and Versailles, and then we went on a European tour that lasted five weeks.

We started off in Germany and saw Munich and the Bavarian Woods. Nestled in the Woods was the resort of Garmisch and the resort of Oberanmergo where the famous *Passion Play* was held. Garmisch was nestled in the mountains near the Zudspitz Peak. During the winter it was a ski resort, but in the summer it was a fairyland of food and water skiing and shopping and local fare. Together, we learned to water ski and went on horseback rides. Stevie bought lederhosen and a Bavarian hat with a quail feather in it and I still have both. We climbed to the top of the Zudspitz and I have a photo of Stevie sitting at the Mount. You could see Austria from the view up there. We dined on oxtail soup and goulash and other German foods; they were delicious. We stayed at the resort for about two weeks and then traveled, by station wagon, to Italy. Yes, we had shipped the pink Chevy station wagon to Paris with us and it was quite a hit with the folks there.

Stevie atop the Zudspitz Mountain in Bavaria, Germany 1959

We traveled over the mountains to Venice and saw all the famous sights one can see. We ate gelato and pizza, which is not the same as American pizza. My father insisted that we have the full European experience and we went to all the churches and museums that Italy and Germany had to offer. We traveled to Florence and Pisa and then on to Rome. We saw the statue of David and the Leaning Tower of Pisa and the Coliseum and the Vatican and the Sistine Chapel and the Pieta. And then we traveled over the mountains again, to the French Riviera. We stayed in Cannes about a week and Stevie was reveling in the sights of the women in bikinis on the rocky beach. We took a paddle boat out onto the bay and rammed an American naval ship, which Stevie thought was hilarious and I was scared to death. From Cannes we traveled to Lourdes and saw the Basilica and the shrine to Our Lady and Mother walked through the waters to heal her broken body as she had a fused spine and back problems. Mother did not travel well and ended up on the train back to Paris, but Grandma and Grandpa Fee took everything in stride and had a marvelous time. The station wagon was crowded but it handled everyone very well and did not break down once but drew attention where ever we went. There was much souvenir shopping on the way and I remember stone fruit and golden tables and leather goods all bought in Florence on the famous bridge the Pont d'Eveccio. I bought Stieff stuffed animals in Garmisch, I remember one in particular, an orangutan. The trip, or the Grand Tour, was one of the most wonderful memories of our life up to then and it was good that it was such a family affair.

We returned to Paris and spent the rest of the summer vacation with our international friends at SHAPE Village. One, in particular, was friends with Stevie. He was Italian and his name was Reno Beraducci. He was very friendly and handsome and they got along very well. We also had an au pair girl from Denmark named Junna. She was very beautiful and was very talented in cooking and sewing and in makeup and cosmetics in general and she was very popular with the soldiers. I think she was looking for an American husband. My mother was jealous of her and after a grand dinner party where Junna cooked and served and dressed to the nines my mother exploded and fired her as the men at the table were not paying attention to anything but Junna. It was quite an evening. It was the farewell dinner for my grandparents and Stevie. All of them were soon to return to America.

After sad farewells, Grandma and Grandpa and Stevie left by plane for the US. Stevie went back to Concord, New Hampshire where Saint Paul's was located for his sophomore year and Grandma and Grandpa Fee went back to Lake Worth, Florida. Lisa was to enter the first grade at SHAPE Village school and I was to become a freshman at the American school in Paris, called Garsch. We three children all spoke French fluently by this time.

Stevie continued to flourish at Saint Paul's. Aside from his academic standing, he ranked in the top fifth of his Form throughout his four years and graduated cum laude in 1961, he was extremely involved with school life and the schools extracurricular activities. He served, with distinction, on many diverse clubs including the Scientific Association, Mathematics Society, Cercle Francais, Glee Club and Rifle Club. He was a writer for the *Horae* and *Pelican* and played in football, hockey and lacrosse. A friend remembers him as being "small in size, but fierce in enthusiasm and determination,"--whatever he undertook he did without fanfare, good-humoredly and to the top of his powers. He continued to spend his holidays with the Wallers and we saw him again in the summer of 1960.

During that summer, the family went on a trip to Eastern Spain, where Barcelona is located, and we took a train to Lluretide Mar which is the busiest and most popular tourist resort in the region. It was very underdeveloped at that time as the war was only over for 15 years and its impact was still felt amongst the people and the land. Eastern Spain covers an extraordinary range of climates and landscapes — Pyrenees in Aragon to the beaches of Costa Blanca and Costa Calida, popular for their winter warmth and sunshine but still relatively unknown at that point in history. Lluretide Mar is located on the Costa Brava which stretches from the French border and is a mix of cliffs, wooded coves, and pretty beaches. When we arrived, there was a holiday going on so the banks were closed and we had only a little Spanish money with us. We could only eat bread and sardines and Mother had brought peanut butter with us. I learned to love sardines at that time and the Spanish bread was delicious and so very fresh and warm. We stayed in a suite of rooms in an hotel near the beach. The beach was sandy and empty. The surf was gentle and the water temperature was comfortable for bathing. Stevie got his first taste for surfing there. My father bought me a navy blue and white bathing suit that I remember vividly. There was no one there but us and a few vacationing soldiers. The family had a wonderful time and then we left to go to Barcelona for a few days. We ate paella which is a Spanish casserole dish consisting of seafood and chicken and vegetables and saffron rice. It is delicious and we all loved it. After our time on the Costa Brava, we drove back to Paris and Saint Germaine-en-Laye.

Waiting for us at home at SHAPE Village was our new au pair girl, Inga. She was young and tiny and very pretty and Stevie was infatuated with her. She, too,was from Denmark. My mother liked her so she stayed for the summer and she and Stevie dated and had a lovely time during the waning summer. In the middle of SHAPE Village was a chateau which was used as a social gathering place for teenagers and young people. There were dances and parties and education classes all the time. Stevie took full advantage of the chateau and he and Inga enjoyed it to the fullest. Reno Beraducci was still a part of our lives and it was a magical time with teenagers from all over Europe there; we all played and danced and mingled. There was also Stevie's friend, John Kerry, who spent his summers in France. He and Stevie went on a bicycling tour of the Bretagne coast. Stevie knew how to get the most out of life and he did. He was a wonderful and loyal friend and brother.

Then it was time for the Sixth Form to start and Stevie returned to Saint Paul's for his senior year. He was dating Donna who attended Miss Porter's

Boarding School, that is how they met. She was tall, taller than Stevie, and slender and pretty and smart and polished. I would not meet her for another year when we met in New York City. Donna was from Kenilworth, Illinois a lovely and stylist suburb of Chicago. Her father was an attorney and her mother was a stay-at- home mom. Donna was a very centered person and she always handled life well and with grace and poise. She had a beautiful smile that lit up the lives of people who saw her. Stevie was accepted into Princeton University and Donna was accepted into Vassar College. Stevie wanted to be an international attorney or work for the Diplomatic Corps. He spoke five languages fluently and was very charming and savvy. Donna would go on to become an attorney after Stevie's death.

As Stevie was graduating in 1961 and my father's tour of duty was three years old it was time to make decisions as to rotation of station or to remain in France for another year, which we could have done. My father decided that the family would return to America in time for Stevie's graduation and we were assigned a duty at Wright-Patterson Air Force Base in Dayton, Ohio. The school year flew by and it was time for Stevie's big day. The family arrived in New York City in June of 1961 and immediately went into culture shock.

Everything was so different than Europe; the train we took to Cheshire, Connecticut did not have windows that came down or private rooms for sitting, the automobiles' headlight beam was white instead of yellow so it hurt your eyes when you were driving, people spoke English which I found to be confusing, and the people's manners were terrible. No one shook hands when you were introduced and they ate with their hands most of the time. Young people did not curtsy when they were introduced and people dressed differently - not as elegantly as the Europeans. Cosmetics were an unpracticed art and life was changed forever. The Wallers' and the Sehls' and the Kelseys' all traveled to Concord, New Hampshire for the graduation.

It was a huge event and everyone was so proud of Stevie as he was awarded the *cum laude* distinction and received the Cercle Francaise award for outstanding writing of a work of fiction in French. Stevie wrote under the name Brandy of K-Bach which was our French poodle's registered name. His award was a magnificent set of red leather bound books containing the works of all the great French writers of the Great Epoch. He received many distinction awards for his extracurricular activities and club memberships, and the family was proud. The day itself was glorious as only a New England summer day can be, and there was not a cloud in the sky. It was a day of promise and hope.

The family spent time in Connecticut with the extended family catching up on life since our leaving three years previously. Then we packed up the Chevy station wagon and drove to Ohio. The summer was spent acclimating to our new world. Wright-Patterson Air Force Base was a prime assignment for Dad and the base was a luxurious one with two Officer's Clubs, indoor swimming pool and outdoor swimming pool, bowling allies and tennis courts, skating rink and golf club and the 18th Hole. The officer's homes were either townhouse in build or single home brick with large yards facing connecting commons. The homes had the best and newest goods and appliances and there was a fireplace in each home. There was a lot of late night partying amongst the youth and cocktail parties for the adults. Stevie was an immediate hit at Wright-Patterson and his best friend was Wood Rigsby the Commanding General Officer's son. His favorite girlfriend on the base was Meredith Krieger who shared a common with us.

Stevie at Wright-Patterson Air Force Base, Ohio
1964

The base was situated in Fairborn which is a suburb of Dayton and it was an impoverished town with no culture or life. It was gray and dismal and it had a lot of car dealerships and fast food places. One was Frisch's which served the Big Boy that I remember as being very tasty. Dayton was about a half hour away and it was a slumbering city with not much to it either. There were two department stores and some movie theaters and bars and a modeling agency which also was a modeling school. Life was not the same at all and I yearned for Paris. Stevie adapted well as did Lisa, but I did not. With the summer drawing to a close Stevie turned his attention to Princeton and Lisa was enrolled at the Catholic school Mary Help of Christians where she was in the 4th grade. I was entered in the Fairborn public school which had the distinction of having the highest birth rate in the state. I was a junior.

1961-1965

1961 was exhilarating for Stevie as he entered his freshman year at Princeton University. He was courted by the exclusive Colonial Club. He joined their organization and moved into the house which was a large white two story building with large round columns and a portico in the front opening onto a large green lawn sweeping down to the street. His major was History and his minor was French. He immediately joined in the extracurricular activities of the school earning a place on the varsity lacrosse team. He made many good friends and I was contacted by one, Karl Ege, who wanted to build a school in Stevie's name and the name of another fallen Princeton hero, Dave Hackett.

The school was to be built in Dong Ha, Vietnam, Quang Tri Province where the Marine Combat Base had stood during the war and where Stevie and Dave, also known as "Moose," were killed in combat. The school was to be named in their memory and to quote, "..many of us have not forgotten the sacrifice these two classmates made 'in our Nation's service and have been searching for a way to remember them in a constructive manner consistent with the values, principles, and commitment embodied by Steve and Dave." The group of Princeton classmates found a solution to their quest in PeaceTrees Vietnam. PeaceTrees was originally formed to clear land mines from the area surrounding the Dong Ha Combat Marine Military Base but quickly grew into the construction of "PeaceTrees Friendship Village," including new housing, a kindergarten, community center and other facilities. The classmates were to construct a kindergarten, an adjacent playground and a soccer field to cost a total of $33,000 all donated by Princeton alumni. The seven classmates, all Vietnam veterans, who spearheaded the drive were: Tom Curto, Hugh Durden, Karl Ege, Jake Jacobson, John Keker, Rob Norton and Griff Sexton. Karl Ege was the point man for the families of Stevie and Dave. The school was named the Kelsey-Hackett School.

Kelsey-Hackett School
PeaceTrees Friendship Village

Karl reported to me that the school was indeed built and dedicated on September 19th, 2002. fifty students began classes immediately. Karl traveled to the site of the school together with his wife and daughter for the dedication and said it was "a personal pleasure to have worked on this project and I am glad that so many of Steve's and Dave's friends participated. They may be gone from our presence for over 35 years, but they remain in our thoughts and prayers as they do in the hearts of their families."

A week after the dedication of the school former U.S. Ambassador to Vietnam and formerly a POW in North Vietnam, Pete Peterson and a group of veterans and US government officials visited Dong Ha and PeaceTrees Village and stated that the "PeaceTrees Village and School Project was singled out as one of the most important steps taken by Americans to reach out to Vietnamese and reverse the legacy of this tragic episode in the histories of each of our countries. Hopefully this will increase the visibility of PeaceTrees and allow it to do more good work in Vietnam." "Rest assured the

Kelsey-Hackett school will contribute greatly to future generations of young people in Quang Tri Province Vietnam....." To date, the Kelsey-Hackett School has educated 600 young children and this coming school year, the year of 2015, it will educate another 50 and so on. It is a most wonderful and lasting legacy.

From another of Stevie's classmates, Beau, I received an email that said that he had been meaning to write for ten years and that he remembered Stevie well. He went on to say, "I think about your brother a lot and honor him and remember him and shed a tear for him through all these years." Beau was one of the contributors to the school project and left a remembrance on the Virtual Wall on Veterans Day, twenty years after the Wall was dedicated. Beau finished his note by saying "that many of us remember Steve and miss him after 35 years and do indeed honor his memory."

Stevie spent his college school vacations with the family at Wright-Patterson Air Force Base where he was very popular with both the young men and the young women. During the summer of 1962 the Air Force Academy Cadets came to the base and took over all the young women, much to the chagrin of the young men of the base. Stevie and Wood Rigsby got hold of a supply of cherry bombs and put together a commando team of young men. In the cover of darkness and at the late hour of midnight swept down on the cadets, who were all sleeping in their housing, and planted the cherry bombs at the exterior perimeters of the housing and set them off hoping to scare the heck out of the enemy cadets. Well, Stevie and Wood and company were successful beyond their wildest dreams, but they also set the housing on fire. They fled into the night. Remember that Wood is the son of the Commanding General of the Base and Stevie is the son of the Second-in-Command. The base AP's (air police) put out an all-points bulletin on the co-conspirators and hauled them in at 3AM. To say the least about this incident it is enough to say that the officer's in charge were not pleased with their sons but thought it terribly amusing. The cadets left the base a few days later and life returned to normal for the young people of Wright-Pat.

Also that summer, Jimmy and Lydia W. came to live with us for a while. Their father, Uncle Duke, had just passed away and their mother, Aunt Katherine-my father's sister, had gone back to school to learn a career so that she could raise her seven children. We had a blissful summer as we all got along well. They remember father as being a saint and mother drinking too much. Actually, the marriage was on the rocks and father spent his evenings sequestered in his bedroom with the door closed and the air conditioner running so he couldn't hear anything and Mother was self-medicating with bourbon and cigarettes. A pattern that would continue for several years, until the divorce. Betty was now in the picture, as she too, lived at Wright-Patterson the same time we did.

Aunt Katherine went on to gain a high level of experience in government civil service and reunited her family and spent many years in Italy as a civil servant. She took her youngest son with her, Timothy, and he came back a grown man with a great deal of sophistication, speaking Italian fluently. Jimmy eventually earned a Ph.D. and worked as a civil servant for the Navy in the government. He worked out of New Orleans but was relocated to Richmond, Virginia, following the hurricane called Katrina. Lydia lived in Richmond as a married southern lady and was, as Jimmy described, the general of the family. All the cousins turned out extremely well with education as a top priority.

In the Fall of 1962 Stevie joined the Rocket Club at Princeton and his photo was in the Princeton paper with a tall and winning rocket. He had been so shy as a youth and now he was joining all sorts of clubs and doing all sorts of sports and extracurricular activities. He had gotten in a fight with Daddy over the placement of his prize winning leather bound books from Saint Paul's. We had inherited an antique bookcase that was just gorgeous and Daddy had it filled with his *American Heritage* series of books plus other books and files of family history. Stevie moved some of the books and files around so he could put in his French books. Daddy was always a bit jealous of Stevie and he and Stevie got into an argument over the books and it ended up in a fist fight. I was so horrified that I don't remember who won. My former husband now has the bookcase and I inherited the books and files minus the French books.

During the Christmas holidays spent at the base, Stevie and I would go to the movies on Christmas; it was a tradition. And there were always rounds of parties and open houses and dining at the Officer's Club with special activities planned for the young men and women. There was ice skating at the rink and Stevie got to show off his skating expertise, he learned to play ice hockey at Saint Paul's.

In the summer of 1963, Stevie was invited to visit Princeton friends in Cleveland. They lived in Shaker Heights, Ohio, a very exclusive part of the state. He was showing off for some girls at the pool of a friend and began a dive off the diving board, a backward dive. He pulled it off except for one problem-his nose hit the diving board on the way down, and broke his nose and bled all into the pool. He was very proud of his battle scar and like to tell the tale. During that summer, he also took me to a jazz club in Dayton to hear the legendary Bo Diddley play the blues. Stevie played piano and guitar so he worked himself up to ask if he could join the jam session and Mr. Bo said "Yes, come on up and play." Well, it was like giving Stevie the keys to the kingdom and he played slide guitar with Bo Diddley that night and his feet never touched the ground. Stevie loved popular music and he introduced me to Joan Baez and Bob Dylan and the Beach Boys and The Kingston Trio. He also knew how to dress in the preppy, the New England way, and he took me shopping for college clothes that summer. We went to Rike's in Dayton. I remember he was intent on finding Bass Weejuns, a loafer from Maine. We never did find them, but, later in life when I lived in Maine I went to the factory in Wilton and thought of that shopping trip back in 1963. Stevie had a charge account with Brooks Brothers Department Store and he loved to wear bow ties. He wore a pink shirt from time to time and I have always loved that look since. He wore crew neck sweaters and oxford shirts and Harris tweed jackets and chinos, and in the summer, he would wear madras. He looked elegant in a tuxedo and in the winter of 1963 I saw him in one for the first time. It was at the Plaza Hotel in New York City where I was a guest of a friend from college who was debuting at the Gotham Ball. Stevie met me there along with his date, Donna S. That was the first time I ever met her or knew of her existence, and we hit it off right away. Stevie and Donna looked like they belonged together, and they were dressed for an elegant evening. I don't remember where they had been or where they were going, but for a brief moment we met in the lobby of the Plaza, and it was a moment of great pride for me. I will never forget it.

Stevie was a junior at Princeton, I was a freshman at Marymount University, and Lisa was in the 6th grade at Mary Help of Christians. We did not know that that Thanksgiving was our last as Air Force Brats as Daddy had a sudden retirement from the Air Force and in the middle of the school year left Wright-Patterson and traveled to Florida to stay with his father, Dr. Harry Ray Kelsey, DVM, and his wife Irene, in Lake Worth. Lisa switched to Sacred Heart School, (the same school Stevie and I had attended in the elementary years), in Lake Worth and rode her bike everyday to school. Stevie took the news in stride and I was sent adrift as my world came crashing down around me as I lost my identity - I had lost my Air Force privileges just as I was learning I had them. Christmas was spent at my grandfather's, Kels as we called him, home. His address was 123 North Palmway, Lake Worth, Florida. My other grandparents lived at 1318 North J Terrace, Lake Worth, so the whole family was together for the holiday. The sudden move from Wright-Pat to Florida plus the early retirement from the Air Force plus being in college in Virginia and not knowing where my family was for several months was very disconcerting for me. Stevie took it in stride. I was depressed and Lisa was doing fine as she had been with our parents during the whole move and knew what was happening.

It was now 1964 and Stevie and I returned to our respective schools and Daddy found employment at TWA which was located within the Patrick Air Force Base network in Brevard County, Florida. They traveled to the county to look for housing and found the family home in Indialantic. It was a white ranch style home with a pool. The exterior of the house had brick on the front near the front door and a large landscaped arrangement with boulders and palm trees. The backyard had an orange tree grove plus a hedge of hibiscus surrounding the yard. It was a corner lot and the address was 201 Deland Avenue, Indialantic. Indialantic is located near Melbourne, Florida, but it is on the ocean side of the Indian River that separates Melbourne from the coast. Our house was one block from the ocean and the beach was famous for its width and smoothness and cleanliness and quality of sand. You could drive on the beach and the water held no surprises such as hidden rocks to cut your feet on. The surf was excellent and Stevie invested in a 6 foot long surf board and began his surfing career. Pierre was still with us though he was getting old. He loved to go to the beach and run in the surf. He was such a great dog and friend.

The interior of the house had four bedrooms and three bathrooms. There was a main living room with a fireplace that had no back as it also was in the family room which was on the other side of the wall separating the two rooms. The fireplace was brick. The main living room opened into a dining room and the front hallway. The family room opened onto the kitchen with an island in the middle of the room. The kitchen had two doorways, one for the dining room and one for the laundry room which held a turquoise washer and dryer and a bathroom. This whole part of the house opened onto the screened in pool area complete with landscaping and tropical plants. The master bedroom and bath had sliding doors opening onto the pool area. My bedroom had windows overlooking the pool area and Lisa's bedroom was the corner bedroom overlooking Deland Avenue and Shannon Avenue. Stevie's bedroom was next to Lisa's and overlooked Deland Avenue as well. It was across the hall from my bedroom.

Deland Avenue was a quiet neighborhood street with little traffic. It was a mile to the center of Indialantic, which consisted of a main street, called 5th Avenue, that ended at A1A and the beach. The main street held the city hall, which Stevie helped to build, some dress shops and that was about it. On the walk to 5th Avenue there was a hotel with a putting green. There was an old hotel built in the Mizner style (which is Mediterranean) and had two floors. It, at that time, was in disrepair.

Lisa entered 7th grade at Our Lady of Lourdes. The school was overcrowded with up to 50 students per classroom. Some of the nuns were described as "battle axes." The school taught kindergarten through 8th grade and Lisa stayed for the last two years. She later entered Hoover Junior High in the 9th grade and then went on to Melbourne High School for the rest of her studies. After the summer break Stevie entered his senior year at Princeton and I entered my sophomore and final year at Marymount as it was only a junior college at that time. It has since grown and is now a four year school with education and nursing teaching as its focus. They now take male students and have boarding facilities. Marymount has partnered with Loyola University and they work together to teach youth and participate in athletic activities.

The 1964-65 school year was well underway and Stevie was reveling in it. His relationship with Donna was growing stronger, his studies were progressing well, and he made plans for the summer— a working trip to Europe. By this time he spoke French, Latin, German, and Greek. He continued with his music instructions, gaining expertise in the piano and guitar. We spent the Christmas holiday together in Lake Worth at Kels's home.

Kels had a beautiful, old style Florida home plus a detached apartment over the garage. We stayed in the apartment over the garage. Pierre was still with us and he had learned to travel and change homes with ease. He was a magnificent dog and pet and family member. It was good to be together for the holidays as the month leading up to Christmas had been fraught with uncertainty as to where my parents were and where would they end up. It was a delightful Christmas and the last we would spend together as a family unit. The next Christmas Stevie was teaching in Melbourne, Florida and I was married and living in Washington, DC. Stevie and I went to the movies on Christmas Day and had respective visitors from school who were visiting the area. Mother was happy to be near her parents, who doted on her, and she was happy to be back in Florida. It was the last family get together we would have as my Grandfather Fee passed away at Easter, on April 25, 1965.

Jonathan Michael Fee was born on September 29, 1888 in Far Rockaway, New York and died in Lake Worth, Florida on April 25, 1965. He was 77 years old. He died of a massive coronary at the breakfast table where he was serving his wife, Marguerite, her breakfast. His Requiem Mass was held at Sacred Heart Church where he was a parishioner. He was interred at Memory Gardens Cemetery, Lake Worth, Florida. He had loyally and lovingly taken care of his wife since their marriage in 1916, 49 years earlier. He left behind his wife, two daughters, Marjorie and Eileen and six grandchildren.

He had so tenderly taken care of Grandma Fee that no one knew how sick she was; she was suffering from the middle stages of Alzheimer's. When it became apparent that she could not live on her own she went to live with Mom and Daddy in Indialantic but she was too sick to stay there and went to live in a nursing home in Cheshire, Connecticut, where she lived for ten years. At her death, she was interred at Memory Gardens in Florida next to her husband.

After the funeral it was time to prepare for final exams and graduation from Princeton and Marymount. There was a great deal of coordinating to be done as there were two graduations and there was a wedding and it all was happening in the first two weeks of June, 1965. The Religious of the Sacred Heart of Mary invited my family to my graduation, to be held at 12:30 on May 31, 1965.

Stevie's graduation was a week long event stretching from June 11th thru to June 15th. The wedding was to be June 11th . Marymount University graduation exercises were held at the school in Arlington, Virginia; Stevie's activities were held in Princeton, New Jersey, and the wedding was to be held back in Washington, DC, in the middle of Stevie's graduation activities.

On June 11th, the Princeton Triangle Club held a play called "*Grape Expectations*" at McCarter Theater; there was a luncheon for The Old Guard followed by The Alumni Parade on June 12th. Sunday, June 13th the Baccalaureate Address was held at the University Chapel, a luncheon for the alumni was held at Upper Cloister Dining Hall, the Senior Debate for the Lynde Prizes was held in Whig Hall, a Service of Remembrance was held at the University Chapel, President and Mrs. Goheen's Garden Party was held with a general invitation extended to recipients of degrees and their families and all who were attending the Commencement and the evening was concluded with a concert by the University Concert Band at Front Campus. On Monday, June 14th,Class Day Exercises were held at Cannon Green, Senior Singing was held at Nassau Hall and the Senior Promenade at Lower Campus between 1901 Hall and Henry Hall. On June 15, 1965, was the Commencement Exercises held at Front Campus.

In front of Colonial Club at Princeton University Graduation 1965

The two weeks began with pulling Lisa out of school for the last weeks of her 7th grade in Florida and driving to Virginia with Kels and Irene. The family stayed at the Marriott overlooking Washington, DC and Georgetown and it was convenient to the school. The graduation was only an afternoon long and my whole Kelsey family was there: Uncle Gene and Aunt Myrtle with daughter, Anne, Irene and Kels, and my parents and my sister. Then they left for Cheshire, Connecticut to stay at Aunt Marj's and Uncle Bill's home with their three boys, Jack, Bob, and Steve. Just as they were settling in, they had to drive back to Washington, DC for the wedding which was attended by my brother and sister and parents and all of my former husband's clan. Then, they had to hustle back to Connecticut to partake of the Commencement activities and graduation ceremony of Stevie from Princeton University. I stayed in Washington, DC and on the 12th of June traveled, with my husband, to Annapolis, Maryland for John's cousin, Mike M.'s wedding and from there we traveled to Maine where we spent the summer. After Stevie's graduation the family traveled back to Florida, splitting up in Indialantic where my parents had moved, and Kels and Irene continued on to Lake Worth. Stevie went to Europe.

1965-1966

To back up a bit, Stevie wrote a letter to the parents in February of 1965 about his plans for the future after graduation that year. He had arranged by the French and German departments of Princeton University an opportunity to work at a bank in Düsseldorf, Germany, for the summer. He also had an opportunity to work in Paris at the bank Societe Generale. He chose Paris. He also had the American Foreign Service job up in the air and said *"If I get it of course I'll even come out ahead, but I won't know till April."* He was strapped for money and asked that his tax refund be sent to him, in the amount of $75.00.

He had a net debit of $343.35 for various laundry bills over four years, University Store bill for that year, and the Colonial Club bill which meant that in order to graduate he needed $300.00. His total income for the year was $843.00. He was searching for jobs for his future career of which direction he was unsure.

In 1965 the Vietnam War had been slowly yet steadily escalating since February of 1954 when the US, under President Eisenhower, offered to train troops fighting "reds" in Indo-China. Vietnam was an unknown country to the majority of Americans. The French had colonized it and were in, what they thought control until the battle of Dienbienphu in May of 1954. Following the French defeat by the "reds" the Indochina Armistice was signed with Vietnam being split at the 17th parallel. The US said it could respect this pact. And there it lay until Vice-President Lyndon Baines Johnson assured Saigon of aid in army build-up. This was 1961 and it is also during this year that American jets flew photo missions over Vietnam.

With rampant corruption and unrest in Vietnam between government agencies, Buddhists and the American's President Diem was slain in an army coup and President Kennedy vowed he would review the Vietnam policy. The year 1963 saw formal ties with Saigon established and in the following year the US enlarged the American force by 5,000 advisers to work with the ARVN (Army of the Republic of South Vietnam) as helpers in the step-up for a prolonged offense. In Washington it was viewed as a show of concern over the trend of the war and in May Dean Rusk warned the "reds" that war in Vietnam may be widened.

So, this is where young men and women were in the summer of 1964. The draft had been in effect since the Civil War and was in use causing these young citizens to be concerned about their future and their welfare. The first draft card was burned with the young dissenter saying, "The basic issue is my right of choice." 1964 marked the end of innocence in America. The cities were in unrest over civil Rights and the murders of Martin Luther King and Malcolm X, the President had been assassinated and we were definitely escalating to full blown war in a country people could not find on a map of the world. America lost her optimism. (Margolis viii).

In 1965, US jets attacked North Vietnam for the first time in reprisal for raids and President Johnson ordered families home from Vietnam. Yet, the President was fearful of alarming North Vietnam's allies, the USSR and China. Thus was put in place his theory and practice of containment, which continued throughout the war. We were not to win, just keep the NVA in their place. The USA admitted to a shift in plans. We were no longer to only "advise and assist" but to engage the enemy –in their territory and keep them there. The President also ordered 50,000 more men to Vietnam and doubled the draft, enraging the populace of the US and the anti-establishment movement was born.

People refused the draft or cited "conscientious objector." fleeing to Canada or ill health as reasons for being labeled ineligible to be recruited. But many young men and women felt duty to their country and the fight against communism which the President stated as the cause for all action necessary to contain the "reds" and not offend the USSR or China. LBJ was the first President of the USA to go to war not to win it - thus failure was built into his plan as Hanoi fought to win. America and Vietnam . (Marrin 88). The objective was to convince North Vietnam leaders that they could not win.

This is the atmosphere that the graduating class of 1965 faced and the dilemma Steve was in. He was a devout American and believed his President and his policies and quoted the "Domino Theory" many times as reason to fight but he was hoping for time: time for graduate school and marriage and a legacy should anything happen to him. But, his time had run out and he was called and he followed as was his duty to his country and his principles. He joined the Marines, something he had been building on for a lifetime.

While in Officer Candidacy School at Quantico, Virginia, 44 sailors died a fiery death aboard the USS Oriskany aircraft carrier in the Gulf of Tonkin where it was anchored with the carriers Constellation and FDR. The President made a surprise visit to South Vietnam to salute his troops and praise them.

For the troops,Vietnam was an alien landscape filled with alien peoples, with extreme heat, insects, snakes, jungles, rice paddys, mountains and booby trapped babies being used as bombs and the unAmerican way of fighting – fighting with no valor just horrific torture and captured soldiers being skinned alive. The troops had left America and were "in-country" a never-never land called "The Nam" (Marrin 122).

Booby traps and mines accounted for 11% of all American deaths and 17% of all American wounds; this did not take into account all those mentally injured by seeing a buddy blown apart. From then on soldiers walked with eyes glued to the ground. (Marrin 137).

In 1967 General Westmoreland was so sure of victory that he dared Hanoi's leaders to make an all-out attack. And so they did. But, the Lieutenant was not there as he was Killed in Action prior to the Tet Offensive. A battle 2/5 fought.

During 1967, in April, anti-Vietnam War protests geared up in earnest and 100,000 rallied in New York and there were many more protests in DC and the West. In May of 1967, Marines began fighting in the "Demilitarized zone" and Steve was there for the beginning. He did not make it out.

He had applied to the Marine Officer Candidacy School – OCS. This was a final ace in the hole. He said, *"I would seriously prefer the Marines (3 years). I'll be taking the Foreign Service test in May — I've already sent in the application. I should get the results in late June or so, at which time I will then have my oral exam (if successful). If in Europe, I can take it there, which might even be better. I've also interviewed here with the National Security Agency. and if I want to follow that (much like Foreign Technology division) further I will have to take a qualification test in the fall (and a polygraph on my sex life!). In a few more weeks I will also be seeing CIA, which interests me more than NSA or TWA (perhaps something in their international department). I've also talked to Merrill Lynch, mostly out of curiosity, and they have a type of junior executive program which doesn't seem bad and which I could probably easily qualify for. If I did anything uncritical like this I would have to look seriously at a six month and military program, although the shaky status thereafter and the years of meetings, I hear, are a great burden. This is the extent of my job hunting."*

He went on to say that his interest lay nowhere else and that he felt no great dedication to any one career at that time as he wanted to go on to grad school and from there enter into a military career.

He also wrote, *"As an aside, I'm beginning to wish more and more these days that I'd given in to what once seemed like adventurism and gone to the University of Miami and studied oceanology. There certainly would have been no question of my future career plans or my dedication to the field —which has always really fascinated me — not to mention the fact that it would have been fun and probably less of a financial burden."*

Concerning graduate school, Stevie said he would like to take the Graduate Exams Records exam in that spring but needed $10.00 for registration. He was really strapped. The Graduate Records Exam came out just before the Foreign Service Exam and it would be good practice for him. He wrote on that his senior thesis was coming along well and that he was relatively interested in it. The weather was miserable, but he went surfing in the Jersey surf with the water temperature at just 38 degrees. He was wearing a wet suit. He concluded his letter with his grades thus far in that semester: Politics B-, Math B-, English History B+, European History B- and overall a B average. He was hoping for better and was disappointed that he didn't do better. He went on to graduate and work in the bank in Paris, France, and he had a magical summer. He was still dating Donna.

During his stay in Europe he sent postcards and letters keeping the family informed of his goings on. His first postcard asks how Mother was doing following her surgery for gall bladder removal and generally how she was doing. At this time she was in a physical therapy ward in Bilouxi for the gall bladder and her spine; she was there three months during that summer. Stevie was very concerned and expressed it by saying that he hoped the operation would ease her pain and that she would be in peace. He concluded the postcard by mentioning Mrs. Jacobs, a Parisian who was also Lisa's Godmother; he said he looked forward to contact with her during his stay in Paris.

In a second postcard he wrote of his work saying it was just alright . He was in export-import transactions. The bank was near a base and he had access to the Post Exchange. He had been invited to Brittany and Nice for weekends by acquaintances and the people at work, whom he described as very nice. He did say he missed the beach however and that is exactly how Lisa was spending her summer vacation before entering 9th grade at Hoover Jr. High School, in Melbourne, Florida.

In a letter, undated but during his stay in Paris, he spoke of business matters concerning his near future, deciding to enlist in the Marines as a Reservist thereby getting around the draft. He also would take the Foreign Service exam, to be held in Washington, DC in late summer early Fall. He said he had lost weight but was feeling healthy, he was down to a size 28" waist on his trousers. He missed meeting Mrs. Jacobs as there was a time lapse in communications but he did go to the theater to see *The Barber of Seville* and two plays at the Opera Comique and they were described as a lot of fun. A club mate appeared in Paris on Stevie's doorstep after a grand tour of the world. His friend's parents had a wonderful apartment on the Ile Saint-Louis overlooking the Seine and the back of Notre Dame. They were planning on spending time together while his friend was in France and before Stevie traveled south.

Stevie was planning on going home to Florida and then taking the car and driving up to Washington, DC for the Foreign Service Exam and then going on to Connecticut to see the northern relatives of which he was very close to. He did stop in Washington and visited with John O. and myself in late summer. He took the Foreign Service Oral Exam and did not pass. He came straight to our apartment and looked dazed and confused. He said the interviewers thought him too stiff and therefore not eligible for the Foreign Service. It was a cruel blow. Stevie said he should have had some beer before going into the exam to relax himself. He was devastated. And, that left the Marine Corps or Graduate School at Florida State University as his only options. He also was writing regularly to Donna and was planning to meet her in DC in the Fall. He sent her a beautiful postcard written in French saying how much he loved her.

He stayed in France and Germany for the summer and continued to write home. He had a strong sense of family and love for this family. He wrote that when he returned to Florida he could drive Grandma Fee, who was staying with mom and dad at Indialantic, Florida, to Connecticut where she would be put in a nursing home as she was too sick for the family to take care of her. He offered but felt he would be refused. He signed off by asking about mom's drinking and her convalescence now that she was back home from Bilouxi, Mississippi.

In a letter dated July 17, 1965, Stevie wrote of his birthday and friends from Princeton visiting and taking him to their villa in Pleneuf, not far from where he and John Kerry used to go. Without transportation the twosome and two girls, friends of his friend, played tennis and swam and ate and had a good, relaxing time of it. Stevie's birthday and the two girls birthdays were during the same week so they had a celebration. Stevie was back in Paris in time for his birthday, which was the same date as the Bastille celebration, so he wrote that he saw the military aspects of the day in the morning and that evening he went to Saint Germaine des Pres for street dancing and supper with a friend from Princeton . They all went to Notre Dame for the fireworks but the fireworks got rained out, disappointingly. He talked about his work and the French banking system as complicated and full of red tape and he mentioned that his French was good enough to pass him off as a Frenchman. He discussed business concerning his life insurance or lack thereof. He spoke of Northwestern Insurance versus GIR Insurance, a government insurance plan. He closed by sending a bonjour to Lisa and hoped mother was feeling better.

On July 29, 1965, Stevie wrote about his life in Paris and his plans to quit his job on the 20th of August and hitchhike to the Riviera and then over to the Atlantic and Biarritz, and then back to Paris, perhaps by way of Brittany again. From there, on to London and home. But his social life in Paris was wonderful and very exciting though the job was boring. He says, *"I've really discovered Saint Germaine des Pres with its restaurants and jazz cellars. I've been to a discotheque to.....the other night I went to Montmartre for the first time since being in Paris this summer and it was quite a view and with all the artists, tourists and beatniks it was very interesting."* At the bank, where he worked, there were student parties on the roof of the Maison, from nine floors up and it was quite a view and fun as well. There were many nationalities present.

He went on to say that he had heard Lyndon Johnson's speech about the draft and he was feeling apprehensive about the draft and his situation. He asked how dad's work at TWA and the missile base were doing and how mom was feeling. He closed on a funnier note with *"Also went over to Les Halles the other night, after the Comedie Francaise, for some soup, crepes and wine w a French kid and some guys from Amherst. Had a great time."* And that was the last letter to be saved so all I can say is that he had a magical summer and it was a summer of apprehensions, as well, over the war and the draft and his future. None of it would be resolved until the Summer of 1966 when he was drafted and joined the Marine Corps.

Upon returning from Washington, DC and Connecticut he became a teacher's assistant at Hoover Junior High, Melbourne, Florida, teaching 7th, 8th and 9th graders. He was a very popular teacher, especially with the girls. In fact, when Lisa went to Hoover the following year as a 7th grader the students who knew Stevie did not believe she was his sister. She says she was a "dork" when she arrived at Hoover, coming out of a Catholic school, but by year's end she had accomplished a major transformation and was very chic and popular.

After completing his year of teaching at Hoover Junior High, he went to Quantico, Virginia for basic training and Officer Candidate School. He sent his parents a card from the basic training facility and it showed his pride and his humor. It went like this: *"Hi there, Here I am at Quantico, Virginia defending you, your loved ones, and our country — Frightening Isn't It? Love, Steve".*

The summer of 1966, June 5th was graduation, and it was hot in the DC area. Donna was living there and they wrote often to each other. John and I were living in DC also and saw quite a bit of Donna and got to know her very well. She was a delight and a perfect complement to Stevie. John and I had moved off of Capitol Hill and moved to Harvard Street in DC located at the back end of the Washington Zoo. Donna lived just at the other side of the Zoo at the front end and I would take Chris, Stevie's new nephew, for walks through the Zoo to see Donna. We got along terrifically. When it was time for Stevie to graduate from OCS in the Marine Corps as a 2nd Lieutenant, Lisa came up from Indialantic, Florida, and we went together to see him receive his diploma and ceremonial sword. It was thrilling and chilling at the same time. He wrote a letter to his father about OCS and reported that the past few weeks had been hectic and he thanked Dad for the watch and the lieutenant bars he had sent although they were Air Force bars and not Marine Corps bars.

He then wrote about Basic Training and how demanding it was. *"Basic school has gotten off to a rapid start.....We'll qualify with the M-14 and the .45, have about 20 other weapons to learn, also land navigation, amphibious assaults, field exercises and lots of physical training and academics."* Then he had some time to himself and he and Donna went to visit Florida at Mom and Dad's and stayed 10 days. Then it was off to California for Stevie and back to Washington, DC for Donna.

Stevie made a cross country trip of getting to Camp Pendleton, California. On the way he saw the Grand Canyon and traveled through Texas and Arizona and New Mexico. He had many trials with his car but finally made it to his new base. He took a leave of absence to spend Thanksgiving with Donna in Illinois and announce their upcoming wedding to be held on January 7, 1967.

He had flown in from Camp Pendleton where he was a student at the Marine Corps' Defense Language Institute at Monterey, California. Donna's family and the Kelsey's were in heaven over the announcement. Mr. Edward W. S. announced the engagement to the press. Much activity began to happen after this announcement as the wedding was to be a very formal affair. Donna's dress was custom ordered at Priscilla's Bridal Salon in Boston, Massachusetts.

The wedding gown was an A-line dress of silk shantung heavily encrusted in a pearl and crystal design and a matching beaded headpiece. Attending her were Miss Joel Ann C. of New York and Stevie's sister, Lisa Bart Kelsey in similar gowns. The 5pm ceremony took place in Union Church in Illinois and then the couple hosted a reception in the Indian Hill Club. Stevie wore his US Marine Corps Dress Blues and looked so handsome and Donna was radiant in her gown. They then went on a honeymoon to San Francisco, California.

In a letter dated December 20, 1966 Steve wrote to Donna about a "great little cottage in Carmel" he had found for them to live in. He was very excited about it and couldn't wait to show it to her. This cottage would be their first and only home together.

1966-1967

Just prior to the wedding ceremony Stevie wrote a letter to Donna, pre-marriage, while in Defense Language Institute. He spoke of missing her and loving her, but his own words speak much better:

Dear Donna,

I'm about to call you, but I thought I would write anyway. Also send along this picture General Masters sent me of TBS graduation. Hope you can stand me in all my splendid ugly. Christ, that bald head of mine has got to go! I can't wait till I can grow my hair long again and hide.

I'm going off my rocker here without you, which is why I think I'll call later. I've really developed a bad case of the blues — I miss you terribly. Nothing I do seems to help. Going away last weekend didn't and I feel even worse after staying here this weekend. Tried to keep busy by surfing, working out, getting drunk and driving around but can't keep my mind off you.

My mood hasn't been helped by the fact that I've been reading "Battle Cry" by Leon *Uris, who was a Marine in World War II. I know you don't read that sort of thing and I guess it's pretty trite, but I wonder if you would get a hold of a paperback copy and read it some time. It's kind of an unofficial Marine 'bible' and it also has some situations in it which are still awfully analogous to our own. It would be helpful to me — it would give you some feeling for the way I've felt about our relationship though perhaps I've never spoken much about it. Which reminds me — I don't think I've ever said it before — how very glad I am that you decided to marry me. Thanks for being patient — I really do love you — and I'll feel much better after we've married even though I'll be going away.*

Hope you had a good Birthday. Sorry I couldn't come up with anything better than a telegram. I really am hopeless in trying to show you proper affection.

Had a funny experience yesterday. Scared the hell out of me when a sea monster surfaced near me. Was actually a bull seal — about 2 tons and ugly but no more dangerous than a porpoise — it took me a while to get over that.

Tried to Christmas shop but no luck. I'm not doing anything right these days. Couldn't even find you a belated birthday present and spent the whole afternoon to get only a little pair of moccasins for Chris. I'm not much good at gifts.

I'll finish up this miserable weekend now by calling you, getting some chow and studying for tomorrow's test. Wish you were here.

Love, Steve

He signed off by writing in Vietnamese *"I love you, naturally."*

In late December he wrote to his parents talking about religion and the actual wedding ceremony, which would not be Catholic. He went into quite a bit of detail about his religiosity and the ceremony and I would like to reprint part of it:

I was surprised when Donna and I first brought up the subject that not too much was said about our wanting the wedding in her church. This does, of course, have certain religious ramifications, and I am aware of them. Before I go on, I'd like to thank both of you for not making an issue out of this because, obviously, I already had made my decision, and I had thought about it. I know it must have been disappointing for you, in particular for Mom and to you Dad since you've certainly done more than your share to encourage me in Catholicism.

In reply to your question, Dad, I have put a lot of thinking in on the subject of religion. That may be the problem! If anything my approach may have been too academic, but at least it has led me to believe that the religious spirit must come from something other than the intellect, is a valid religious concept if the idea 'religion' has any meaning at all. And, that, basically, is where I am now — without the spirit, 'immature' if you will, but at least not anti-religious. I still respect religion very much, have not yet crossed myself off the list, and indeed look forward someday to finding my niche within it, perhaps still Catholicism. I've thunk all I can on it with impasse (I hope temporary) the results and I think that's all any God could want of an imperfect human.

At any rate, I didn't want to set up a Catholic ceremony, because I don't think I could guarantee to the priest all the things the Church would like and I really don't feel any the worse for it.

A second Catholic ceremony here would be a nice idea and I suppose it could be set up with a little pre-verification. But for me it would be only as religious as the wedding at Donna's church and for the Church not all religious, merely ceremony, though the priest might not know it. Not very respectful really for such a hallowed old institution. I think I'd rather wait for the moment when I might really want a Catholic ceremony — which is not yet a complete impossibility. It would be even nicer then.......Please don't feel that the wedding will be second-class, religiously speaking, as you may have guessed from the above, I still count myself as rather a religious soul, if non- defined, and the wedding will have a certain deep significance for me, as I'm sure it will for Donna.

The letter went on to talk about his Vietnamese language studies and he said the language was easy to learn and he had aced the first test.

He never had time to find his religious identity as he was killed six months later. I don't know if he ever found the inner peace and contentment that come from a deep and abiding faith in God. He was given a military funeral service with a Liturgy For Catholic Masses in the chapel at Fort Myer, Arlington National Cemetery.

After the wedding and honeymoon, Stevie and Donna settled down to military life at the Presidio in Monterey, California where Stevie attended the the Marine Corps Defense Language Institute. On the 16th of February, 1967 he graduated from the Institute as the outstanding graduate of the Defense Language West Coast Branch in his class. There was a photo and article about Stevie graduating from the Institute. The ceremony pictured was the Pacific Grove, California Kiwanis Club award being given to Stevie by Ronald Gibler, chairman of the Chinese International Affairs Committee. He had a Marine Corps bald head and was wearing his khaki officer uniform.

In March, he started training and things were really confusing. Donna and Stevie went on vacation near Lake Tahoe and went skiing and the weather was just right for the young couple to play and have fun. "Lots of good weather, scenery and excitement." They had moved from the cottage in Carmel to a beach side home in Oceanside and they were enjoying it tremendously. He said that he would most likely be flying from there on April 10, 1967, by way of Hawaii and Okinawa. Donna would probably go back home again for awhile, but would also go to Washington and Florida. They would sell the car that had given them so much car trouble and he would ship his gear back to Florida. Their address in Oceanside was Apartment 22A, 1202 North Pacific Avenue, Oceanside, California.

Before shipping out to Vietnam on April 10th Stevie graduated from the Naval Amphibious School in a course titled "Reconnaissance Unit Personnel

Supporting Arms Training" and the date was April 7, 1967. On April 19, 1967, Stevie sent a postcard to his parents saying he had cleared Hawaii in an hour and would arrive in Okinawa soon. He had sold the car and put Donna on a plane just before he had left California. On April 24, 1967, Stevie wrote a note to Donna saying he had not been put in Reconnaissance but was sent to the 2nd Battalion, 5th Marine Regiment, and he thought he "was out of the kettle". He had time to do some shopping in Okinawa and had bought a tape recorder which he had already used and had sent a long tape to Donna. His company was called "Foxtrot" or 2/5 as the company was known and "Foxtrot" returned from battle and was returning to Battalion headquarters the next day for a few weeks so Stevie would have a chance to "get my feet on the ground." He signed off by saying he hoped Donna's teachers interview went okay. She didn't get the position.

Foxtrot 2nd Platoon
kneeling on left Cpt. Graham on right Lt. Kelsey

At the end of April, Foxtrot had gained a significant edge over the enemy in the An Hoa valley and western part of Go Noi island, as a result, the company was eager to go out on search and destroy missions. After the April 14th engagement, Lieutenant Colonel Mal Jackson sent the company to China Beach for R&R, as the soldiers had performed so exceptionally well. Stevie talks about this trip in one of his letters to Donna.

On the 9th of May 1967, Stevie wrote to Donna in response to letters and photos she had sent to him. He was delighted with all the correspondence and he said the photos *"damn near turned me on. My wife is so pretty it makes me burst with pride!"* He went on to discuss her options for work in the coming year and stressed that she should look for work that she could get out of quickly as in December he was going to Okinawa and would send for her and she could live there while his tour was played out. They were living on a small budget which is what they both wanted. Monthly income was limited to just $150.00 per person for both of them. Then he went on to talk about his time in Vietnam and said that so far it wasn't too arduous. He feared more for her brother, Tod, and his motorcycle, than he did for his own life. A few memorable events had happened to him since his arrival there and he went on to say:

I helped a Platoon of combined Marines and Viets (combined action) get set up in a nearby Ville where three months ago the VC had entered one night and murdered nine of the villagers. I gave them a plan of defense and helped them coordinate and speak with each other and it was very interesting. Yesterday with about ten minutes notice I took my platoon out about four miles from here to a bunker some of the locals had found full of mines and booby traps that the VC had stored there.

We took some samples but it was too dangerous to probe the nest so we blew it. The populace had cleared the area, which is a bad sign, so we made it back here without further incident. We worked closely with the local people and the chief on this and they seemed quite relieved when we successfully completed the mission. Just a few days ago I brought my Platoon back for three days of an in-country R & R at China Beach near DaNang. Would you believe I actually surfed there, and am now a member in good standing of SEASA, the Southeast Asia Surfing Association! Rest and relaxation with a few suds thrown in was all they had there, but the troops enjoyed it, though I must say I was glad when it was over and I could stop being den mother to that bunch of beach bums.

We aren't involved in any operations now, though we may be shortly. On the whole Charlie seems content to stay clear of the big ones though. It's usually a single squad that gets in trouble, and I never go out with less than two.

The little problems are more bothersome than the big ones. Somebody falling asleep on post or getting into some other mischief and looking after the troops is an endless task, as well as manning the perimeter while we're here.

until next time. Love, Steve

2nd Lt. Straughan D. Kelsey Jr.

In a letter dated May 17, 1967 he wrote to his parents about his Marine Corps gear that he had to carry and the problems with fighting a war in Asia. He spoke matter-of-factly about these hardships, hardships that would crumble a regular solider--- but not a Marine:

Dear Folks,

Haven't had a chance to write for a while as I"ve been on operation. Am leaving again in an hour or so and am not sure when I'll be back again. Have been doing a lot of 'humping' in mountains, waist-deep streams, rice paddies, jungles, through heat, dysentery, blisters, etc. and am getting quite tired but at the same time used to it all. Have also been out advising AVN forces several times. As you can see the load we carry is heavy — toilet articles, four meals, 60mm ammo and 81 mm ammo (mortar rounds) *and two canteens but we're well equipped in case of enemy contact, which by the way has been light so far. We also wear helmets and flak jackets of course.*

Hope you have a good anniversary trip. Thanks for your letters and the photo of Chris, he sure is cute. I've sent along a present, but it may come late so be looking for it. The pictures are for Mari and Lisa, the slides you can have developed to get a look at the area here.

Much Love, Steve

The gear the Marines wore to battle

On the same day and during the same break in operations Stevie wrote to Donna as well. He talked of the same things he had mentioned to the folks but went on to write:

Had a bad case of food poisoning a while back but couldn't afford to let it stop us — nearly killed me in the process. Together with the heat, the blisters, the dysentery and the heavy load it's a wonder how we manage to keep going and yet I don't feel I've reached my limit yet and in fact am probably stronger now than when I started (and skinnier!).

It may be some time before I have a chance to write again so until then take care.

I love you, Steve

Captain James Albert Graham, his immediate superior, had led them through the mountains. Captain Graham was a Christian and a non-smoker and non-drinker. He read his Bible every night and was very highly regarded as a Marines' Marine and superior officer. He had been accepted into the astronaut program but wanted to finish his tour of duty in Vietnam first. Many of his peers believed he was on the fast track to becoming a general officer. Vietnam would cost him his life.

On the 23rd of May 1967 Stevie wrote to Donna one last time. In his letter he makes mention of Operation Union, the Operation that would led to Operation Union II and take his life only nine days later. His letter reads, in part:

Dear Donna,

I just got back from our latest operation and also just got your letter. We got back a little quicker and more successfully than I thought we would. The Company climbed for two days over a mountain range down into the back end of a little valley on the edge of our TAOR (Tactical Area of Responsibility). *When we got to the valley floor (after many heat casualties, and thank God I'm in shape) I finally found out why we are here. We could observe gooks running around in uniform with helmets on. We found out later, they had a stronghold on the valley, schooled the local people and taxed them and billeted their people with them.*

The valley was lush with food everywhere — water, tons of rice, bananas, pineapple, water buffalo, etc. but the people had been quite impoverished by the VC levee's. In fact, they were operating quite a little Garden of Eden. Before they could react to our presence we began sweeping with my Platoon on the point. We swept the whole afternoon for many miles and through many villages. When it was over we had 16 VC kills, including their gear, packs, helmets, cartridge belts, grenades, etc. and had hit them so quickly that they hadn't had a chance to inflict a single casualty, which around here is something like a novelty.

So, so far the Platoon has 16 confirmed VC and no casualties and it's a hard bunch and fast acquiring a reputation as the best platoon in the best company in the best battalion in the Corps. As for the VC, we found from interrogation of the locals that they were strangers, some NVA, who had filtered back into the valley from Operation Union, attested to by the fact that the dead were still lying where *they fell when we pulled out a day later — highly unusual in a local guerrilla situation — nobody had bothered to pack them up.*

The letter went on about financial details and talking about a fellow Marine, Michael, who was loaned to Operation Union II. He was a friend of both Donna and Stevie and he also dated Elysee, Donna's best friend, and there were plans that they all would spend the time together in Okinawa in December. Michael would find Stevie's body ten days later in a rice paddy in Vinh Huy, Quang Tin Province, Vietnam.

The last letter written before his death was to Mother, wishing her a Happy Birthday and Happy Anniversary. He inquired about her health and convalescence. The card was dated May 31, 1967.

In their book, *Battlelines*, Lieutenant Colonel David B. Brown and his daughter, Tiffany Brown Holmes, wrote of the battle of Operation Union II and the time line. This is what they wrote as taken from survivors and records of that dreadful day:

"Millbrook Six (referring to Lieutenant Colonel Hilgartner), this is Fox Six, over', he began. 'Roger Sir. I can't send my company across that large rice field unless I prep the area first. I need air or arty support, over.' Graham insisted.

The Marines of Fox shared surprised, slightly angered looks as Graham pleaded his case. 'Maybe so, Sir, but that prep fire was a long time ago, over.'

Hilgartner's response was quick in coming.

'In that case we need to get up on Hill B to set up our own machine guns to provide cover, over,' Graham countered. His Marines exchanged stunned glances with one another. Why wouldn't the Battalion give them air support?

'I spoke to Delta Six before he came under fire, and he said he didn't get this far south,' Graham argued. 'Yes, I know Delta's getting heat up over there, but unless we get some support right now we'll get beat up as well, over.'

Graham was silent for a moment. 'Well, at least let me have one round of arty to register,' he remonstrated. If the artillery battery was able to hit its objective accurately with one howitzer then,when called to do so, the other howitzers could also act immediately and accurately by using the same registration data.

'Aye, aye, Sir,' came Graham's final, tight lipped reply.

Gunnery Sergeant Green and Lance Corporal MacKinnon registered the disgust in Graham's tone.

Graham stared at nothing, managing his frustration. To no one he blurted in disbelief, 'He just gave me a direct order to move out.'

Green and MacKinnon understood the captain's frustration. Direct orders were given only to subordinates when they did not understand or were tending to refuse the direction of the senior. Not complying with a direct order had the most serious consequences. However, there was no question in the minds of the three of them that complying with the direct order without prep fires was tantamount to suicide. Never the less................Graham turned, 'Mac, get me the actuals,' he said referring to his rifle platoon commanders: Second Lieutenant Schultz, 1st Platoon; Second Lieutenant Kelsey, 2nd Platoon; and Staff Sergeant Marengo, 3rd Platoon," (Brown 93-94).

This quote from the book, *Battlelines,* set up the scenario for the disadvantaged Marine Battalion. After describing in detail other aspects of the battle, in which 39 Foxtrot soldiers lost their lives, the authors go on to write about Stevie and his part in this tragedy:

'Hey, Sheehy, tell Fox Six that the 1st Squad just bagged fifteen NVA in the paddy in front of Hill A,'Second Lieutenant Straughan Kelsey mentioned to the radio operator. With that, the last of the 2nPlatoon began entering the dry flat rice field to begin searching the fallen NVA soldiers. The soldiers appeared to be quite young.

Heavy, their packs were filled with rocket-propelled grenades, RPGs, AK-47 munitions, and 82mm mortar rounds.

By the time the entire 2nd Platoon was fifty meters into the rice paddy and had peeled off to the left, the company command group entered the scene. The rice paddy, now clearly visible to Graham, was 350 meters deep. It ran left to right about 450 meters across. The tree line directly in front was obviously the hamlet of Vinh Huy, Fox's objective. Along their entire left flank was a hedgerow of bamboo trees. On their right was another hedgerow of bamboo trees, but, unlike the first, this one did not enclose the entire field. This hedgerow stopped about seventy-five meters shy of the hamlet and exposed another 600 to 800 meters of rice field, somewhere close to where Delta was fighting. Graham recognized his company's huge vulnerability, and it pressed down upon him like he was Atlas, the weight of the world on his shoulders.

Finally joining the 1st and 2nd Platoons, Graham directed First Sergeant Lee to move the wounded prisoners to the rear of the company column to the 3rd Platoon's location and get the POW's ready for choppering out to the rear. 'Top, stay with Staff Sergeant Marengo. I'm taking Painter and LaBarbera with the CP. If you need me, call me on the radio.' 'Aye,aye, Sir. Good Luck.'

The pitched battle up in Delta Company's area continued. As Fox moved forward cautiously, Delta's fight served as a gruesome omen for the men of 2/5. Rounds that strayed from Delta Company engagement flew overhead or landed in the rice field near the Marines. Fox's unit leaders shouted orders, 'Stay down if you are not involved with the POW's,' (Brown 97).

After some time the battle grew closer to Steve:

13:50 hours. "The company began its trek across the rice field. The 1st and 2nd Platoons were on line each with two squads forward. The Marines readied themselves for resistance as they grew closer and closer to the line of bamboo trees masking Vinh Huy, their ultimate objective. Due to the shape of the paddy on the left, the 2nd Platoon neared the tree line from almost 200 meters away while the 1st Platoon, perhaps 250 meters from it, approached from the right," (Brown 99).

14:20 hours. "In the heat of the tropical summer afternoon, the NVA initiated their attack with unrelenting bursts of machine gun fire from the tree line that stood directly in front of the 1st Platoon. Another machine gun fired from an area with a small pagoda on it located in front of the 2nd Platoon. Within a millisecond, fifty to one hundred automatic and semi-automatic arms were unleashed upon them from the bounding hedgerows in front. A machine and two automatic weapons on Hill B fired on them from behind. B-40 rockets roared four feet above the paddies impacting on the far side. Another .51 caliber NVA machine gun, located on Hill A, opened up twenty seconds later. Mercilessly, it fired into the backs of the 2nd Platoon. A torrent of 82mm mortars rained onto the rice field and the trapped Marines. The enemy machine guns in the Vinh Huy area had a low angle of fire that failed to impact on the paddy, instead, they grazed the grasses twenty to thirty inches above it. The machine gun on Hill A, however, fired in a plunging angle, spraying bullets down upon the field and the entrapped company.

Through the wall of lead, men of the 2nd Platoon instinctively launched their final assault attempting to gain superiority. Lance Corporal Gobrecht marveled at Corporal Jerry Westfall, the squad leader on his left, who charged the machine gun position with M-16 at his hip while making some wild charging yell. Racing forward Gobrecht glanced right toward the other infantry squad. Firing, men dropped even as they ran. He glanced left. Westfall had been cut down. Large holes opened in their line. The brave men from the 2nd Platoon no longer able to sustain any assault, one by one, dove belly down and hit the paddy as they continued to fire. The deafening snap of bullets at the air above them.

The NVA mowed down both the 1st and the 2nd Platoons. Many made it to a prone position without being wounded. Some did not. The dead were still. The mortally wounded lay helpless, dying on the rice field. The slightly wounded remained frozen, calling out to see if their buddies were still alive. Only the two-foot high dikes and the poor angle of fire provided any safety from the deadly guns.

The killed and wounded littered the field. Second Lieutenant Shultz, 1st Platoon Commander, lay mortally wounded. Shultz's Platoon radio operator, Corporal Lloyd Woods, realized that his lieutenant was exposed to the intense enemy machine gun fire, and jumping up, made a mad rush through the splattering of lead projectiles to reach him. Once there, he hoisted the lieutenant onto his shoulder and lumbered both of them to a safe position behind the dikes.

Then, rallying his four companions, Woods sprinted across the open rice paddy attempting to evacuate another wounded Marine he saw lying near an enemy machine gun. When he reached the wounded man, Woods realized moving him would be impossible because of the enemy gun fire. Ignoring a spurt of inaccurate machine gun rounds, the corporal crashed into the tree line towards the enemy. The gunner, in total awe at Wood's reckless aggressiveness, failed to shoot at the charging Marine.

Woods fired his M-16 until he was out of bullets, killing the stunned NVA. He picked up the NVA machine gun and leapt into the adjacent emplacement taking out the second gunner. Using the enemy gun on other hostile positions, he provided cover for his companions to allow the other Marines to evacuate their wounded men. Corporal Woods wasted no time returning to the field where Fox's wounded lay and organized their evacuation. The two machine guns in front of the 2nd Platoon continued to spit rounds at the men.

On the left flank of the Platoon, Corporal Victor Driscoll's squad was the closest to a machine gun that fired from an island of bamboo trees that seemed to jut out from the tree line masking the objective Vinh Huy. This area was conspicuous because a small Buddhist pagoda used by rice farmers to pray during the harvest season was located there. Driscoll's squad could not assault the gun because the machine gun they were up against supported a lethal trajectory and was well fortified. Overwhelmed, the Marines leapt up to their feet and fled back towards Corporal Ted Varena's squad. Lance Corporal Art Byrd was gunned down while he made his escape,"(Brown 100-101).

The battle intensified and many were gunned down. The battle was not over however and at:

15:15 hours. "Marengo assisted with the triage activities for wounded brought back by Corporal Nutt's squad. As Long's squad assaulted the NVA entrenchment at the summit from the back of Hill A automatic weapons fire rang out from on top of the hill. They killed six enemy. All of Long's Marines sustained at least one wound. While men were setting up a hasty defensive position, Long spotted another machine gun that was firing on the 2nd Platoon further down the face of the hill. He charged the gun. Two Marines attempted to stay up with their magnificent, athletic squad leader as he again led an assault on the second gun. Bullets ripped across the heavy air, now laden with gun smoke. Long ignored the racing projectiles as he would have ignored flies. Two more enemy went down. Long, along with the other two Marines, was wounded again. The Marines at his side crumpled from their respective wounds again. Long rushed forward, attacking as he moved. He fired, overcoming the NVA manning the machine gun nest.

Long stood alone as Hill A fell silent.

Below, Graham and his eight men, their lungs heaving with the effort, reached the 2nd Platoon area. In front of Graham, existed an island containing the pagoda. From the far side of the rice field, the bamboo trees on the island. Particularly with its long axis paralleling the hamlet, made the island appear to be tied into the hamlet.

'Skipper, Hill A's machine guns are quiet,' Gunny Green panted.

'Great. Long must have taken the hill, Gunny.'

'All right, men,' Graham said to all, 'when that next air strike comes everyone who can, get up and assault that gun near us on our right. That's the one right past the pagoda. We have to yell as loud as we can to scare them.' The men nodded at his idea. 'Okay, I hear a jet coming so get ready on my command.'

The Marines steeled themselves and awaited his command. 'Let's go!' he shouted," (Brown 106).

15:35 hours. "With gusto and much bravado, a group of eight Marines and one corpsman began their charge. Their war scream frightening, Graham led the way. Within forty-five seconds, Captain Graham, Gunnery Sergeant Green, Lance Corporal MacKinnon, Corporal Dirickson, Lance Corporal Painter, Private First Class LaBarbera, Second Lieutenant Kelsey, Corporal Barnes, Private First Class Jack Melton, and six others crammed themselves into the left side of the bamboo tree line near the pagoda. Green took the front of the charge, killing ten NVA himself.

Lance Corporal Gobrecht and two others from the 2nd Platoon pushed onto the right side of the island while firing at the retreating enemy A sniper hidden at the base of a nearby bamboo tree dropped the two Marines running beside him. Gobrecht ran through the tree line firing his machine gun at all bamboo tree root systems until he ran out of ammo. Grabbing three grenades one at a time, he threw them in any other location he thought might hold a sniper. Freshly dug fighting holes and tunnel entrances seemed everywhere. Out of ammo and deep inside the underbrush Gobrecht came face to face with two armed NVA soldiers. Instant fury shot from Gobrecht's eyes. Panting like a wild bull, his breath came in short, almost shallow bursts. His teeth gritted as if he was about to devour the two Communists. Shocked and staring at the fearless Marine, they backed away quickly, fading into the brush. Gobrecht turned slowly assuring himself they were truly gone, then hustled back to the pagoda.

The ruins of a French built home lay near the pagoda. Its intact structural walls served as the protective barrier for one of the machine guns that had all but wasted the 2nd Platoon. Now, thanks to the stalwart efforts of the brave men of Fox, as led by Lt. Kelsey the gun position had been overrun and captured. Some of the 2nd Platoon busied themselves with rendering the gun useless. Corporal Barnes and Gunnery Sergeant Green organized the table and wounded men and formed a hasty defensive position. They had gone without water since noon. Gunny Green knew he couldn't do anything about their dehydration; instead he had the Platoon redistribute their ammunition.

Graham finally made radio contact with Lieutenant Colonel Hilgartner to announce that he had taken a portion of the objective. Dirickson was by his side. Barns, Gobrecht and Corporal Gary O'Brien, another 2nd Platoon squad leader, rested nearby. Graham claimed the opportunity to call First Sergeant Lee and directed him to send more men and ammunition.

'Lieutenant Kelsey, get a group together to silence that other gun.' Graham ordered.

'I need volunteers to go with me to get that other gun. Who is interested?' Kelsey asked.

Immediately a chorus of 'Count on me, Lieutenant!' sounded from the remaining Marines. Among the volunteers were Corporal Francis, Private First Class LaBarbera, Lance Corporal Painter along with five other Marines. They left the pagoda area, traversing safely on the rice paddy side of the island to its end. From there, they hovered nearly twenty meters away from the hamlet's true tree line. Kelsey charged first as Francis, Painter and LaBarbera stayed with him while the others from the 2nd Platoon veered right," (Brown 106-108).

Lt. Kelsey took the island and was charging with his remaining men around the island when they saw a large number of NVA coming at them. That's when they thought they might be in some trouble. It was at this rounding of the island that Lt. Kelsey was struck by a bullet in the back of the head and fell backwards into Cpl LaBarbera's arms and died instantly.

Lieutenant Straughan Downing Kelsey, Jr. was born to be a Marine. He is a hero and his story has never been told.

He was deployed to the 2nd Battalion 5th Marine Regiment 1st Marine Division as Lieutenant in Command of 2nd Platoon – Foxtrot. They were assigned to Quang Tin Province in the Que Son Valley at An Hoa Marine Combat Base.

His regiment, and in particular his Platoon, were called to fight Operation Union II on June 2-3, 1967. The battle, which was a search and destroy mission, took place southwest of Da Nang in the Que Son Valley. This location was the hub of the Ho Chi Minh Trail, the Delta Region rich in agriculture and the Trail, and the Viet Cong meant to maintain that route at all costs. They were waiting for Fox company on June 2nd and Operation Union II quickly became a massacre.

During the battle, Kelsey had been assigned to take a pagoda which was on a hill in the middle of a rice paddy at Vinh Huy. The Marines were outnumbered but didn't think much of that as they were Marine fighting men and Lt. Kelsey, along with this Platoon, crossed the rice paddy evading spider traps (holes in the ground with enemy hiding waiting to spring up and kill) peppering the field. Lt. Kelsey's steadfast courage inspired more Marines to follow his lead. It was without fear of his own safety that he upheld the honor and devotion to duty. After moving halfway across the rice paddy, the North Vietnamese Army opened up with devastating machine gun fire cutting down over half of the Platoon within the first few minutes. Lt. Kelsey was subjected to withering fire and ambush from two entrenched North Vietnamese machine guns. They were approaching the pagoda when Pfc. Dennis Sheehy was wounded in an artery in his upper arm/shoulder. Lt. Kelsey, whose M-16 rifle had jammed, stopped his approach to minister to him, wrapping his own belt around his shoulder to stop the bleeding and thus saving his life. Lt. Kelsey then resumed his charge with his remaining men, holding up his pants with one hand and firing with the other.

Lt. Kelsey and Sgt. Rick Barnes then went around the hill and saw that there were several hundred Viet Cong coming at them. Lt. Kelsey, holding up his pants with one hand (due to loss of weight attributed to the food poisoning a week earlier) and firing with his other, led his men into the fray and it was at this time that he was killed. He was shot in the back of the head. He was 23.

The survivors say of him that they cry for the loss of such a great man who could have done so much good for the world. Pfc Sheehy is quoted as saying, "He tried to save the lives of his men, he was courageous under fire. There were a lot of brave Marines that day and Lt. Kelsey was among the bravest." Sgt. Barnes concurs, "I once knew a great man."

The Marines of Foxtrot distinguished themselves conspicuously by gallantry, intrepidity, and extraordinary heroism on the day of battle, June 2, 1967. Kelsey is remembered for his leadership, compassion, inspiration, duty, bravery, and uncommon valor as shown on that day in that battle that was Operation Union II.

Tom LaBarbera, a survivor of that massacre, wrote to me to tell me his memories and this is what he said of Stevie and the battle:

Firstly, I was assigned as a clerk with Fox Company from April, 1967-April, 1968. I think I joined the Company a week or so before your brother. I had volunteered to go out on Operation Union II which started at the end of May, 1967. Your brother, Steve, was the 2nd Platoon Commander at this time. I am sure you got the details from Dave Brown but it was a terrible day start to finish.

After getting ambushed that morning with 2nd Platoon being in the middle of it literally we finally got to a small pagoda area where the paddy workers would have their meals and rest. It was there that your brother led a small group of Marines beyond this position forward to find and silence dug in enemy who that day were North Vietnamese Regulars. I found myself at the end of this group and when we finally set in your brother was about 2 or 3 feet in front of me. Sadly, Steve was killed with *the first burst from the enemy, I think instantly. The rest is really superficial. Many men died that day. Hopefully knowing how Steve died will bring some relief or closure to you and your family.*

Because I was in the office I got to know most of the men in the Company and I remember Lt. Kelsey as a gung ho young Marine officer who was well liked by his men, because he led by example.

The only other thing you should know is that the date of the this battle was June 2nd not the 3rd. I don't know how it got confused but it was definitely the 2nd." June 2, 2009 Tom LaBarbera

On the website thevirtualwall.org a remembrance is made to Stevie and a thought as to the date of the battle. It states that the battle occurred on the 2nd and the bodies of both the Marines and NVA were searched for and recovered on the 3rd. There were so many casualties on both sides that both sides sought their dead in peace and in accord at the same time. The reason that the dead Marines were listed as being KIA on June 3rd was that their bodies were retrieved on the 3rd of June.

The following is the correspondence sent to Donna informing her of Stevie's death while on Operation Union II in Quang Tin province.

"2nd Lt Straughan D. Kelsey, Jr. 094828 USMC
'F' Company, 2nd Battalion, 5th Marines

Received gunshot wound to the head from rifle fire resulting in his death. The Commandant of the Marine Corps sends his deepest sympathy. You will receive a telegram from Headquarters, U.S.

Marine Corps, Washington, DC confirming this report."

On June 9, 1967 a telegram was received by Donna, who was back in Illinois,and it said:

"I deeply regret to confirm that your husband Second Lieutenant Straughan Kelsey Jr. died June 3, 1967 in the vicinity of Quang Tin, Republic of Vietnam. He sustained a gunshot wound to the head from rifle fire while on an operation. His parents have been notified. The following information is provided to assist in making funeral arrangements. His remains will be prepared, encased, and shipped at no expense to you, accompanied by an escort, either to a funeral home or to a national cemetery selected by you. In addition you will be reimbursed an amount not to exceed three hundred dollars toward funeral and interment expenses if interment is in a private cemetery, one hundred fifty dollars if remains are consigned to a funeral home prior to interment in a national cemetery, or seventy-five dollars if remains are consigned directly to a national cemetery. Please wire collect Headquarters Marine Corps your desires in this respect, indicating the name and address of the funeral home or national cemetery to which you wish the remains sent and whether or not you desire an escort. The Rock Island National Cemetery, Rock Island, Illinois is nearest your home. Letter will follow concerning circumstances of death. I wish to assure you of every possible assistance and to extend the heartfelt condolences of the Marine Corps in your bereavement. Wallace M. Greene, Jr General USMC Commandant of the Marine Corps."

A mutual friend and soldier of Donna and Stevie's who was serving in Vietnam and was involved in Operation Union II came upon the scene after it was over and this is his report. The officer is named Lt. Richard J. Long, Jr. (Michael) USMC, 2nd Battalion 5th Marines 1st Platoon 'E' Company and he is writing to his girlfriend Elysee, a friend of Stevie and Donna. The letter was written June 5, 1967:

"Dear Elysee,

By now you know that Steve is dead. The only thing that I'm going to tell you is what his First Sergeant told me, 'He died like the Marine that he was'. We fought our way to them and saved some of them but he was dead.

Life goes on Elysee and don't you ever forget it. Donna must be proud and live so he would be proud of her. He told me before Union II that if he ever died he could say that he had lived life to the fullest with her and he could die happy. He told me that he was the luckiest man in the world.

Life does go on and it will for you and I. No sweat my lady. You do your half of it and I'll do my half and the twain will meet and that I promise you.

Well I have to man the lines tonight so I'll be cutting it here. Take care and keep a stiff upper lip. As we say over here, 'You must lean into it and be harder than most.'

My love to you, Mike"

Back at An Hoa in his tent were found a book of Shakespeare, a chess set and a photo of Donna and Chris – his nephew who he knew.

Stevie was 23 years old.

Following is a partial list of those Killed In Action that day:

Captain James A. Graham, Frostburg, Maryland (Medal of Honor)
2nd Lieutenant Straughan D. Kelsey, Jr., Indialantic, Florida
Sgt. Gerald L. Ackley, Dunnigan, California
LCpl Richard L. Blasen, Wheaton, Illinois
LCpl Arthur M. Byrd, Houston, Texas
LCpl William S. Dougherty, Evansville, Indiana
Cpl Victor M. Driscoll, Bellaire, Texas
LCpl Gary W. Kline, Lincoln Park, Michigan
LCpl John R. Painter, Palmdale, California

LCpl Jereld E. Wespthal, Bethel, Kansas
Pfc Larry N. Boatman, Caddo, Oklahoma
Pfc Jimmy R. Crook, Austell, Georgia
Pfc Lawson D. Gerard, Santa Monica, California
Pfc Michael D. McCandless, Columbus, Ohio
Pfc Dennis E. Monfils, Riverside, California
Pfc Keith M. Moser, Lowell, Massachusetts (Silver Star)
Pfc Robert Richardson, Augusta, Georgia
Pfc Clifford Shepherd, Dayton, Ohio

Total Marine Rifleman losses on Union II from May 26th to June 2nd were 110 men killed and 241 wounded. With 32 Marines killed and 39 wounded on June 2, 1967, Fox 2/5 reportedly lost proportionately more of its men for a single day of combat than any other American infantry company during the entire Vietnam War.

Several letters were returned to sender following his death. Among the letters returned was one from Donna in which she says she had received the tapes Stevie had made and the sound was excellent and he sounded like himself and that she had gotten all his letters but wasn't sure he had gotten all of hers. She had settled in Carmel and said it wouldn't be the same with him overseas. She continued to look for a teaching position but was getting desperate and was thinking of becoming a waitress. Stevie never got the letter. Also returned was a letter from his father dated May 30, 1967:

Dear Steve,

Well we have our big flag out and our Blue Star hanging in the window, so guess we're all set for Memorial Day. Enclosed is a poem I thought you might like, tho'--as I recall-- the interest of the troops is less academic than this.

We didn't go to the Virgin Islands after all. Lisa had had hay fever and we just don't trust the bigger kids too far. It's good we stayed, however — I have a chance to get acquainted with everyone again.

Keep your powder dry.

Love, Dad

The poem is lost to time.

There were innumerable letters of condolence sent to both Donna and his parents. The President of the United States, Lyndon Baines Johnson sent a letter as did the Governor of Illinois, Otto Kerner, Congressman Donald Rumsfeld, W. C. Westmoreland, General United States Army Commanding, Donn J. Robertson Major General, USMC Commanding Wallace M. Greene, Jr. General, USMC Commandant of the Marine Corps and Richard J. Long Colonel, Artillery Commandant-Commandant of the Defense Language Institute.

The funeral was held at Arlington National Cemetery in the old section near President Kennedy's grave site. Stevie was given a funeral with full military honors, including Taps, a 21 gun salute, a horse-drawn caisson led by a riderless horse with a boot in one stirrup placed backwards.

The loss was so great to the family that they never recovered. The dysfunction that was always an undercurrent in the family came out in full colors and devoured the family. A light had gone out and it would never be re-lit.

Donna was given an allotment by the government for Stevie's death and used it to go to law school in Chicago, Illinois. Donna wore bridal colors, a white dress, to the funeral.

His favorite meal was eye of the round roast beef, medium rare, peas and mashed potatoes.

WHAT THEY SAW AND SAID

Tom LaBarbera 2/5

While assigned to Fox Co 2/5 during June 1967 I was on Operation Union II. I was attached to the headquarters Ptl. During the battle that day; our 2nd platoon was the point platoon of the company. Lt. S. Kelsey was the platoon commander of 2nd platoon. They were pinned down in the middle of a large rice paddy. Headquarters platoon commanded by our commanding Officer Captain James A. Graham tried to get to 2nd platoon to take some pressure off of them. While advancing toward them we worked our way beyond their position into a small pagoda area where we were able to regroup.

By the time I arrived into the pagoda area there was a small squad being formed to go beyond this area to engage the enemy who had retreated about 60 yards beyond our position. This squad was lead by Lt. Kelsey. We were about 7 or 8 Marines from 2nd Platoon and headquarters personnel. Lt. Kelsey was the only officer with us. He took the point and lead us into a treeline where we took up defensive positions. When I got into position Lt. Kelsey was in front of me half in and half out of the treeline - he had been fatally shot while setting up the position. The two Marines on either side of me were also killed.

I was not at the pagoda area when plans were being made for this assault but I am sure that Lt. Kelsey volunteered to lead this group so as to try to silence the enemy. His actions that day were heroic and selfless.

All the other members of that squad were killed either in that treeline or subsequent to it. Captain Graham was also killed soon after in the pagoda area. The other staff NCO Gny Sgt. John Green was killed in a car accident some years after he returned home. My account of that day is still fresh in my mind as I feel it will be forever.

I am sure that considering the facts and that Lt. Kelsey accepted this assignment knowing full well the consequences of his decision to lead this squad, the decision to put him up for a commendation is long overdue.

Please feel free to contact me if I can be of any other help to you.

Thomas P. LaBarbera April 1, 2011

Testimony Supporting Recognition of Lt. Straughan Kelsey for Bravery and Leadership

June 2, 1967 During Operation Union II in South Vietnam

Submitted by: Dennis Patrick Sheehy

I, Dennis Patrick Sheehy, have been contacted by Ms. Marianne Kelsey Orestis concerning details leading to her brother's (2nd Lt. Straughan Kelsey, USMC) death on June 2, 1967. Lt. Kelsey was commanding the 2nd platoon of Foxtrot Company, 2nd Battalion 5th Marine Regiment during Operation Union II in the Republic of South Vietnam. The following testimony is as correct and complete as I remember.

I arrived in Vietnam as as PFC around March 23, 1967 and was assigned to Foxtrot 2/5 as a rifleman. Later I "volunteered" to serve as a radioman for Sgt. Gene Ackley (the platoon guide). Lt. Kelsey joined Foxtrot sometime prior to Operation Union II, which for Foxtrot occurred between 28 May and June 3, 2967. Foxtrot 2/5, commanded by Captain James A. Graham, was op-conned to the 1st Battalion, 5th Marines for the operation.

On or about the 28th of May, F 2/5 was flown by CH-53 from An Hoa Combat Base to join 1/5, I believe we spent two nights at that location prior to being flown by CH-46 to a landing zone in the Que Son Valley to commence the operation. During the initial part of that phase of Union II, I don't remember any serious contact in which 2nd platoon was involved. I also interacted infrequently with Lt. Kelsey during this time as I was carrying the radio for Sgt. Ackley.

On June 2nd, following a couple of incidents involving the NVA and the 2nd platoon (i.e., one Marine in the 2nd platoon was wounded and medevaced, and approximately 10 NVA/VC were engaged as they crossed a rice paddy to our front), Foxtrot, with the 2nd platoon leading, assaulted across the same rice paddy towards a treeline and hill on the opposite side of the paddy.

In the assault, Lt. Kelsey and half of the platoon were in the lead, and about half of the platoon, including myself, was further behind. When Lt.

Kelsey and the lead elements of the platoon were about 2/3 of the way across the paddy, and Sgt. Ackley and the remainder of the platoon were about ½ way across the paddy relative to the opposing treeline, NVA dug in at the treeline and on the hill firing with machine gun.

The time was about 10:00AM on June 2nd, 1967. Instantly, there was a high number of casualties in the 2nd platoon. Sgt. Ackley and I weren't hit during the initial contact and went to ground alongside a paddy dike about 50 yards from Lt. Kelsey. I remember Sgt. Ackley trying to get the machine gun going, but the gunner (Johnson) yelled back that he had been hit in both legs and that the gun was inoperable. After a period of time, Lt. Kelsey called me over the radio and told me to tell Sgt. Ackley to have Marines under his control move towards him. I think his plan was to consolidate the remainder of the platoon to try to suppress fire from the NVA in the treeline. With the order from Sgt. Ackley, two Marines (one was a black Marine named Sheppard) moved towards Lt. Kelsey, and were almost immediately wounded (one of the men survived, the other died of his wounds). Following this action, Lt. Kelsey ordered me to bring my radio to his position. I successfully made it to Lt. Kelsey's position, but Sgt.. Ackley was killed as he tried to move to Lt. Kelsey's position.

At this time, I remember there was Lt. Kelsey, myself and two or three other Marines together in one spot behind a rice paddy dike (about 12" high). Also there were 4 other Marines behind the same dike approximately 50 ft. from Kelsey's position. (Two of the Marines in the second group were Tom Dickinson, who survived the battle and lives in Northern California and maroon Derickson, who I think was the wounded Marine that Captain Graham stayed with when he was killed). We spent some amount of time behind this dike while Lt. Kelsey tried to radio for air strikes or artillery. I do remember that at least one air strike on the NVA to our front was made that afternoon.

Sometime later Lt. Kelsey made the decision to assault through the rice paddy with the remaining Marines of the 2nd platoon. I think that he made that decision because our position in the paddy was untenable. If I remember correctly, he told me that "we might as well take some of the NVA with us when we died." I remember Lt. Kelsey telling the Marines separated from us by about 25 yards to follow his lead in assaulting the treeline.

Lt. Kelsey told me to follow him, and got up and took off at a run for the treeline. As he was running, he was firing his M-16 at the treeline. I was about 5 yards behind Lt. Kelsey.. As we came to another paddy dike approximately 25 yards from the NVA treeline, Lt. Kelsey went to ground alongside the dike when I was wounded (a bullet shattered my right arm between the elbow and the shoulder).

After a few seconds, Lt. Kelsey called over to me (I was about 10 feet from him) wanting to know if I was OK. I responded by telling him that I had been shot, and that I was bleeding badly. Lt. Kelsey crawled along the dike to me, took off his belt and used it to bind the arm together and slow the bleeding. He also tied a field bandage around my arm. Lt. Kelsey then told me that his rifle has jammed and he was without a weapon. He also used the radio to try to contact more help but apparently was not successful. During this period I remember bullets impacting the other side of the dike behind which we were laying.

After approximately 20 minutes Lt. Kelsey took my rifle and continues the assault on the treeline. I observed Lt. Kelsey successfully completing his solo assault to the treeline, but that was the last time I saw Lt. Kelsey. After he disappeared in the trees, I did hear firing and yelling, followed by silence.

About an hour later, Capt. Graham's command group made their assault by me into the same area of treeline. One of those Marines (a Cpl. Richie) came over to me, and took the radio from me. Later I heard several Marines run by me back towards the treeline from which the assault had begun that morning. During the following night, I crawled on my back away from the treeline because of the close proximity of napalm and gunship strikes. In the morning, after being fired at four times by a sniper, I made it back to the hill where the remnants of Foxtrot were. I remember talking with the company Sgts. (maybe Top Lee) and was then evacuated.

In retrospect, I can affirm that Lt. Kelsey was as fully in control of himself and the platoon as the situation allowed, that he was trying to relieve pressure on his Marines in any way that he could and that his leadership during chaos and confusion never faltered. I feel that Lt. Kelsey is most deserving of at least a SILVER STAR award. His bravery, and leadership, even at this late date, should be acknowledged and rewarded.

Dennis Sheehy March 31, 2011

I, Louis "Rick" Barnes, write this letter in response to a phone conversation I recently had with Marianne Kelsey Orestis. Marianne has requested any eye witness information I have about her brother, Lt. Straughan D. Kelsey and his actions during the battle of Union 2 on June 2nd, 1967.

It was not until my recent phone conversation with Marianne that I did not realize Lt. Kelsey was not awarded the SILVER STAR along with myself for his actions in the leadership of the Marines during the battle of Union 2.

I, Staff Sergeant, Louis "Rick" Barnes had been in-country for 15 months by the time of Operation Union 2. I was serving a six month extension of my first twelve month tour in Vietnam.

I had recently been promoted to platoon commander of weapons platoon and was assigned to the company command group with Captain James Graham in command of the company.

Our first contact with the enemy was in a rock formation during the early morning hours of June 2nd. The automatic fire from a AK-47 sent PFC Yeauter rolling down a large boulder. Yeauter with 3 gunshot wounds across his chest, was sucking air into his lungs from the holes. Shouting for c-ration cigarette packs, I used the cellophane from the packs to seal the holes in Yeauters sucking chest wounds. Instantly he began to breath somewhat normal. Moving up the boulders, Cpl. McAnally, shouted that an NVA was right next to me behind a large rock formation. A grenade instantly exploded wounding both myself and Cpl McAnally in our arms. Throwing a grenade around the boulders, I silenced the Vietcong. After checking the dead NVA, I ordered Cpl. Golbrecht to move his machine gun team up and eliminate the additional Viet Cong fleeing down the rock formation.

It was at this time that I moved down to Captain Graham's position. Captain Graham stated he was instructing Lt. Kelsey to move his 2nd platoon into an assault position. He was to advance against the NVA on the other side of the rice paddy.

Captain Graham instructed me to move down with Lt. Kelsey, that he could use my help.

Moving down to the paddy, I advised Lt. Kelsey that I would be on his left flank with two of my machine gun teams.

After moving halfway across the rice paddy, the NVA opened up with devastating machine gun fire, cutting down over half of the platoon within the first few minutes.

Laying in the rice paddy Cpl Golbrecht and Cpl Gary O'Brien were to my left and Lt. Kelsey was directly to my right. With Lt. Kelsey's radio man shot and my good friend Lance Corporal Westpahl dying in my arms the decision was made to assault the tree line. We were not going to lay there and watch more of our Marines dying in the rice paddy. We assaulted the same time as the command group.

Lt. Kelsey, myself and Cpls Golbrecht and O'Brien assaulted the machine gun bunker directly in front of us. Lt Kelsey's steadfast courage inspired more Marines from the second platoon to follow his lead. It was without fear of his own safety that he upheld his honor and devotion to duty inspiring all who witnessed his actions on that afternoon of June 2nd, 1967.

After silencing the first machine gun and many NVA in front of us, Lt. Kelsey and myself formed a small fighting force of some 20 Marines, under the command of Captain Graham.

Another machine gun was now laying heavy fire into the remaining Marines from a tree line on the other side of a short open rice paddy.

Lt. Kelsey turned to me and stated he wanted two men. He went on to state he was going to flank the second machine gun in front of us. It was leading this second assault on a machine gun position that Lt. Kelsey was cut down by heavy enemy fire and sustained fatal wounds.

As the Vietnamese assault continued the command group dwindled. The radio men were dead, Lt. Kelsey had been killed assaulting his second machine gun position and Captain Graham was now shot thru the left shoulder. With the NVA obviously closing in, Captain Graham stood with his radio slung over his right shoulder speaking into his handset. The Captain's rifle was hanging from his wounded left shoulder and his pistol was holstered to his leg.

With myself now hit several times from grenade, mortar and gunshot wounds, Golbrecht also severely wounded, we lay at the feet of Captain Graham. Also laying next to us was Cpl Dirickson, severely wounded in the stomach.

All of the wounded only a few feet from Captain Graham listened to his last radio conversation with the air support, as the jet pilots roared overhead.

"How does it look from up there?"

"Fox six you are about to be overrun."

"Hundreds of NVA are forming for an assault."

"When they get on top of us drop your heat."

"Did you say on top, Fox Six.?"

"Affirmative, Sky Rider, say again to confirm, drop your heat on top of our position. I say again; when we are overrun, drop on top."

It was the decision to drop the bombs on top of our position, that would later keep a Vietnamese officer from shooting me in the back of the head.

Corporal Dirickson sitting upright, despite the fact he could not feel his legs, began tugging at Captain Graham's bloodied fatigues, "What do I do Captain Graham?" Dirickson voice desperate, "I can't move my legs, what can I do?"

Captain Graham glanced at Doc Donovan, Donovan was the only Marine still with us that wasn't wounded. Graham then ordered Donovan to try and get back across the rice paddy. Graham then stated, "I am staying with my wounded."

With lines of camouflaged enemy helmets approaching, and the Marine jets beginning to make their run, Captain Graham un-slung his rifle from his wounded shoulder and handed it to Dirickson and simply asked, "Do the best you can Marine."

As I lay alongside the pagoda, which Captain Graham was leaning against, I watched Captain Graham stand up and firing fearlessly with his pistol into the advancing enemy, and Dirickson sitting upright trying to unjam the Captain's M-16.

With both arms broken at the wrists, I lay unable to fight back. Doc Donovan had refused to leave and lay next to me.

A Vietnamese officer walked up to Doc Donovan and shot him in the back of the head, execution style. As the officer turned to me with his pistol to my head, I heard the ear shattering roar of a Marine jet drop its bomb load within yards of my position.

Nobody moved for what seemed like hours in the mud, blood shattered jungle, among the dead and dying American Marines and North Vietnamese.

When I came to, I realized that Golbrecht was still alive and still beside me. Darkness had fallen over the battlefield and the only sound was the

Vietnamese language, the moaning of the dead and dying, I lay there listening to the single gunshots as the Vietnamese walked through the fallen Marines ensuring every American was dead.

It was only because of Golbrecht and my wounds being so severe that we were both left for dead. It was not until early the next morning that I was medevaced out of the battle zone.

I spent the next three months at Great lakes Naval Hospital and never had the opportunity to speak to anyone from the 5th Marines of the valor I witnessed that day, including the valor of Lt. Kelsey.

It was while at Great Lakes Hospital that I received the SILVER STAR for my actions on June 2nd, 1967

18 March 2011

A Remembrance of Steve Kelsey

There are some people in life you just like the first time you meet them. That was my experience with Steve Kelsey. I couldn't tell you when or where our first meeting was, perhaps sometime during freshman year, but he was the kind of guy you just liked and would have described back then as a "good guy." The image I have of him in my mind is of my coming across campus heading to Blair Arch and seeing him come up the walk and our just smiling and saying hello. He made you smile. He made you glad to see him. He was just like that.

The irony is that we were not roommates or club mates. Nor would we have described each other as among our close friends. But I remember him well, even after all these years, and I honor him and weep for him when I visit his name on the Wall in DC or think of him on Veterans Day. And if he left this impact on me, I wonder how much greater his impact must have been on the family and friends to whom he was closest.

So Steve, I think of you often. And I am honored to have known you. You are truly one of the good guys.

Beau Carter
Class of 1965
Princeton University

Marianne Kelsey Orestis

201 Deland Avenue
Indialantic, Florida 32901

7-21-67

His Excellency The President
The White House
Washington 25, DC

Dear Mr. President,

The war in Vietnam needs give and take, restraint and patience. This is not an endless need, however, and there is a point of which "give" and "restraint" become a loss of our objectives. This point appears to have been reached in Vietnam.

We are not winning, we seem to have no plans to win and we seem quite content to let our one-time allies join in our kill.

In these circumstances, and as both a citizen and the father of a son killed in Vietnam, I feel it my duty to write to you and my right to receive intelligent and informative answers to the following questions:

1. *We seem to avoid winning, even tactically. Why? What has happened to the concept of pursuit and destruction of the enemy? Why was there no pursuit after Union II? Why none after the loss of 74 Army troops in another recent confrontation? Why were the Marines ambushed severely twice in three days in the same place recently?*
2. *Why does each day begin like a game of checkers – set up the new men to be killed in the confrontation and then back to camp for the weekend?*
3. *Why is North Vietnam sacred and safe from ground combat while South Vietnam is so hospitable to invasion? Who are we afraid of? If we must invade to win – and we must – hasn't the time for invading arrived?*
4. *These one-time allies (when they needed help) are helping to frustrate a quick and decent end to the war – why must we sacrifice American boys to retain their goodwill? They have nothing to offer us except trouble. Let us consider America first.*
5. *You are aware of the Rand studies on effective use of various weapons in South East Asia. Why ignore them?*

Mr. President, war <u>is</u> hell and the best way to fight it still <u>is</u> a good offense. As as nation, we must accept this in our innermost being as did the 12,000 dead in Vietnam and get with stopping the bloodshed. My son's blood, spilled there in a rice paddy, challenges all of us at home to have the moral courage to match their physical courage, to win the military victory and set the peace, to save the honor of our country and the lives of our sons, to compromise them no longer. Sending more troops – more cannon fodder is at best an inadequate solution when what is needed is to untie the hands of the combat troops already there and let them win the war – and they can do it. At least, it is a shameful coverup for a cringing US policy.

Because we believe in the above and that America still is great, we have had published the attached ad. We believe that the ideas expressed in 1776 are worth <u>winning</u> a war and peace for.*

We pray that you will act in agreement.

Sincerely,
SD Kelsey

* *Above mentioned ad has disappeared so is not included in this retelling of a father's sorrow and frustration*

Lt. Straughan D. Kelsey, Jr., USMC

Memorial Service

August 25, 2012

It's an honor to be with you today to remember the service of 2nd Lt. Straughan Downing Kelsey, Jr., USMC.

As Americans, we place a high value on our freedom. This freedom, however, does come with a cost. In times of conflict, our country asks some of its citizens to risk their lives on behalf of the rest of us.

Like many families in Maine and across our nation, the Kelsey family answered that call to military service, and sent its son to fight in Vietnam.

Lt. Kelsey proudly served his country as a Marine, distinguished himself in combat, and in June of 1967 he was mortally wounded in a fire fight in Quang Tin Province. Today we honor his bravery and his heroism..

Kelsey – I want to thank you and your family for sharing the proud legacy of your brother. Today's ceremony is a fitting tribute to his service, to his memory, and to all who served in Vietnam.

Those willing to give their strength, their courage and even their lives so that others might live in peace are the noblest of our citizens. They and their families can rightly expect our society to give them the honor they so richly deserve.

And that's why we're here today – to pay solemn respect to that sacrifice and to that honored service.

Thank you for the opportunity to assist in obtaining Lt. Kelsey's military records, which enabled today's presentation of Maine's Gold Star license plate.

As you know, we've placed a request for his medals and will present them to you as soon as they are received.

Congressman Mike Michaud, D-ME

The medals were received along with an American flag and the solemn playing of Taps at his Memorial Service. The most important medal being that of the Purple Heart.

ON BEING A MARINE

Stevie wrote of many things about Marine life that are described beautifully in the Leon Uris novel, Battle Cry, the unofficial bible of the United States Marine Corps. Stevie had written in a letter to his wife of 6 months that she should read it. I don't know if she did but I did and I would like to share my findings with you. My brother wrote in his letter about marching, dysentery, sweating, strain and the agonies of the battlefield. The details of Stevie's letters can be found in Leon Uris' masterpiece.

Stevie was not a soldier he was a United States Marine and he was proud of it. He made many sacrifices to become a Marine and Leon Uris tells why:

"They're a queer breed. You and I will really never know what makes them tick. But if I was on the fighting lines fighting for my life and I had my choice of whom I wanted on my right and my left, I'd call for a couple of Marines, I suppose they're like women....you can't live with them and God knows you can't live without'em." (Uris 330).

Stevie mentioned in one of his letters to Donna that he had found out why they were there. He had found a valley full of North Vietnamese and it was a lush Garden of Eden. The people who lived in the valley were exploited by the North Vietnamese and Stevie felt very deeply about their plight:

'I only hope I'm fighting for the right thing, Marion.' 'You have to feel that way, Danny, or you can't fight'." (Uris 398).

As to marching, Stevie wrote of marching up and down mountains and streams and rivers. He had blisters and food poisoning and dysentery during these marches and in Battle Cry Leon Uris writes of a practice hike, a forced march led by the Company Commander, Major Huxley, affectionately known as Highpockets:

".....Miles fell away. The pace, for a march of this length, was the fastest I had ever seen. With every break I dropped to the roadside for a gulp of water and a quick smoke and eased the heavy pack for a few minutes. It was my feet, though, that worried me. With each break the pain became sharper. When we hit the road it was agony for the first ten minutes. Then the pavement pounded them into numbness. By noon chow I felt like I was walking on a bed of hot coals.

We gulped down the hard biscuits and hash and realized for the first time that we were hungry. We made a fire and heated the coffee. It felt grand going down. I did a quick patch up job on my feet; the two heel blisters were as big as quarters and ready to pop. I cut around them and let the water runoff and swabbed them down with iodine, then ripped a pair of skivvy drawers and folded them tight so the pad wouldn't slip, and put on three pair of dry socks and laced the shoes on tight.

For twenty minutes after the chow break the entire column limped. It was especially noticeable in Sam Huxley. He was a big man and it was twice as hard on him. His feet hurt; I knew it;and it made me happy. Huxley tried to disguise the limp for our benefit by stepping up the pace immediately.

The men cursed and fumed the miles away. Up and down they beat a tattoo on the never ending road. My foot troubles made me less aware of the other pains that were shooting all over my back and hips and neck. Soon they caught with my feet. I felt like a hunk of raw liver going through a meat grinder. Another mile..another.and another. I got short-winded, a thing that rarely happened to me when hiking on level ground. I closed my eyes and prayed. I couldn't quit! What would my boys think? Some were worse off than me and they hung on...I've got to hold...I've got to, I thought.

Every step became unbearable. I felt like screaming for a halt. After each break I was afraid to stand up. The history of my life came before me. How the hell did I ever get into this mess? They wanted to send me to Communications School as an instructor. Why did I turn it down?...I'm an asshole! One more mile gone...another...Manakau...Oahu...thank God!

We swung off the road into a big field.

I wanted to drop on the spot but there was work to do. A communicator's work never ends. We had hiked so well that Huxley pulled us in early for a long night's sleep before the final day's push. None of the platoon had fallen out yet but they were a nightly beat-up bunch. It was an effort to cram down chow and set up for the night. The air was calm and the evening mild and peace settled on the shelter halves in the meadow.

An hour and we were rested enough to sit around and bat the breeze and enjoy a late smoke before taps. As we talked I cut blisters and mended feet. The sick bay was overcrowded and I was blister artist in my own right. I laid out the wet clothes in my pack to dry and buttoned up for some much needed sleep before the big push.

Speedy, on the way to taking over watch on the TCS, came over to me. 'Er, Mac...'

'How's it going?' I asked.

'I think that goddamn Yankee is out of his head. Glad we got only one more day of this.'

'Well,' I said, 'when it is all over we'll be pretty proud of ourselves.'

'Tell me, Mac, and be honest. Did you guys ever take a forced march in the old Corps like this one?'

'Lots of times, Speedy, but I guess the one you are on seems like the hardest. I don't think I'll ever forget this one for a while.'

'Look, Mac, I got a few minutes before I take over the watch. Could I tell you something confidential?'

'Sure, I got my chaplain's badge.

'I don' t want it out that I said this but I saw Levin pull off his boondoockers. His feet are bloody. Maybe you ought to take a look at them.'

'He'll come around to sick bay if he needs help,' I said.

'Look, Mac,' Speedy continued uncomfortably, 'I asked Pedro. He didn't check in. Maybe you'd better let him ride the jeep tomorrow. He can have my turn.'

'He'll get his own turn and no more.'

'Aw, for Christ sake, Mac, his boondoockers are soaked with blood. I know about all the trouble, but...'

'Speedy, Levin won't quit. He's got something to prove.'

'To me?'

'Why don't you just forget it and get on your watch.'

Huxley pulled a fast one on us. He cut our sleep short and roused us at four in the morning. It was pitch dark except for the light of a quarter moon and the stars.

Groggy and bitter we broke camp and with a bar of chocolate we were on the highway in less than forty minutes. It was his plan to catch us half asleep so that the pace and pain would only be half felt. It worked. As we passed the town called Levin we were all in a stupor, like the rest of the column. There were a few halfhearted cracks about the link between Jake Levin and Levin Township but it was a sad attempt at humor.

Only knowing that the end of the hike was in sight kept me going that day. I felt the most miserable and pain filled bastard alive and for the first time in my years as a Marine I was ready to throw in the sponge. I just didn't have any guts left. Huxley had pounded them out of me. I was like a punch drunk fighter, battered and almost out, only staying on his feet because the bell would ring soon and they could drag him to his corner. Foxton might be past the next hill or around the next bend.

For the first time we were not going parallel with the railroad. The route cut into hillier ground past Levin. The rising sun looked down on a gang of dazed zombies tramping and limping up the road.

With each break we gathered our guts for another last surge. Maybe another hour would find us at Foxton. Then another break and another. But Huxley showed no mercy. I pitied any poor bastards who ever set out with the idea of beating our time. And still the miles came and went. The early starting time would cut out the hour stop for noon chow - another Huxley innovation.

Let them try to beat us, crazy bastards, let them try. Let the sons of bitches kill themselves out-hiking Huxley's Whores. I don't suppose a man knows how much he can take. Many times in the hours before daylight I had felt I had reached the saturation point. Yet, each crisis passed and I was still half galloping along at the murderous pace - and nearly all of us were still on our feet

Levin's agony gave us renewed courage. I couldn't order him to stop. The secret had to be kept, even if it killed him.

By 11:00 we began to sense that Foxton was close. The point broke out, almost double timing,in search of the town the name of which was now synonymous with Hell and Heaven. Hell to get there and Heaven to be there. By noon, houses cropped up along the roadside and at last from the crest of a hill we saw her dead ahead. The last two miles meant nothing now. It was almost anticlimax as we trudged through the streets of the sleepy farm town amid greetings from the citizens gathered at the windows and along the sidewalk. We went right through Foxton and were on the highway again.

I was seized with panic! Huxley might want to walk them to Palmerston North! I wouldn't put it past him. The murmur in the column quelled as it swung off onto a dirt road and into a fenced-off field near the ocean.

Highpockets was wreathed in smiles as he checked the time. Of course there was work, but it didn't seem so hard now. It was all over and we were relieved and damned proud. We slowly set up a camp, attended to our dilapidated feet, and a much needed mail call came through.

Aching but happy the battalion settled down. Spanish Joe borrowed a few chickens and a pig from a nearby farm and we had a fine barbecue. A day's rest, a short field problem, and a return by truck to camp were in order. After a songfest around a campfire the boys decided they needed a little liquid refreshment in Foxton. Seabags reckoned it would be mighty un-neighborly to walk up this far and not meet the local citizens. Our area was tightly guarded but Seabags was way ahead of the game. He had taken some message center armbands and planned to walk through the gates while 'testing' the new SCR's for distance.

I wanted no part of it - only sleep. But I made them promise to watch the Injun and keep him from tearing the place apart. As I buttoned down they were already at the gates, cruising past the guards and giving phony test calls on the radios.

Doc Kyser limped into the command tent angrily. He snarled at Sam Huxley. 'Have you lost your mind?' he shouted.

'Come in doctor. I was expecting you.'

'Huxley! I've sat by before on some of your little expeditions and said nothing. This time I'm putting my foot down!'

'Don't put it down too hard, it's probably sore.'

The Doc bent over the table and pointed his finger under the skipper's nose. 'Are you mad? You can't hike them back to Russell. We lost twenty coming up - you'll hospitalize the entire battalion.

Don't pull any crap on me.'

'Don't worry, Doc,' Huxley said. 'I promised them three day leaves if we can beat our own time back to camp.'

'This is it. I'm going to the top. This is the last torture session I sit by and watch. I'll get you court-martialed if it's the last thing I do.'

'Sit down, dammit!' Huxley barked.

Kyser sat.

'If you can't take it, get the hell out of my battalion, Doc. We're in a war. These boys have to be tough. Yes, I'll drive them and I'll drive myself but I'll see to it we are the best outfit in the Marine Corps. Not a man in the Second Battalion is going to be a straggler, not a man is going to die because he is weak. Get the hell out of my outfit if you don't like it!'

'Yes.'

Kyser arose. 'I've got a lot of work to do.' He turned for the tent flap.

'Doc,' Huxley said softly. The medic turned and lowered his eyes. 'Sometimes I don't like myself very much...this is one of them. I have to do it for these boys, Doc...you understand that don't you?'

'Yes,' Kyser said. 'Thank God the Marines are filled with crazy officers like you. Maybe we would never make it otherwise, I'd better go.'

We were thunderstruck! The word passed like wildfire. Surely it was someone's idea of a bum joke. We had hiked in the rain for him; we had given him his record - it just didn't seem believable.

Then it dawned on us that it was no joke. Huxley was walking us back and striking for faster time. In the confused shock of the announcement a vicious anger such as I had never seen mounted. Till the last minute I prayed for a reprieve. The men snarled into their gear.

There was only one small compensation: Huxley would walk too. The point vowed to set a pace that would make even the iron man fall to his knees.

This crazy desire to bring Huxley down was just the thing he wanted. He knew that he would have to throw us into a passionate rage to bring us up to the task.

The first day going back we were so goddam angry that we half ran, throwing all pain and caution to the winds. The pace was brutal and each step was matched with a foul curse along the column. Epitaphs flew, with our feet, southward. I had never seen men drive themselves so hard.

Each break stimulated the insane desire to walk...walk...walk...walk...I didn't know if the squad could stay that way. The beat, beat, beat of leather on the paving might well beat our mood to jelly.

The end of the first day found us ahead of our former time. We cursed right through Levin and tramped to a spot between Ohau and Manakau. A brisk evening breeze came up and men began dropping with chills and fever, puking their guts out. Malaria was swooping in wholesale. We walked till dark and finally set up in a meadow outside Ohau.

Our nerve was quelled. A sudden shock of complete exhaustion hit the battalion. The men flopped and floundered and passed out in the shelters like invalids near death. Only a maniac would try to out-hike the miles covered that day - unless they had Huxley's brother for a skipper.

The second day was different. A nightmare. The emotional burst was spent and now there was the reality of water and pack and road and pain and feet - what was left of them. Physical torture such as I had never felt before. Limping and groaning, we hit the bastard road after a breakfast of a chocolate bar. Every man in the Second Battalion called for the last ounce of strength that God gave him. The column began to fall apart. By noon we were moving at a snail's pace.

Several more went down with malaria. Spanish Joe collapsed, done. During the break there was a ghostly stillness as we sat in the shelter of trees eating our ration. Huxley's purpose was going to backfire.

Huxley needed a miracle. There was a day and a half to go. At this rate he'd be lucky to walk in with fifty men. His purpose would be defeated.

We hit the road. Huxley limped like a cripple. His body looked all out of proportion and he trembled with each step. The word passed down the line that he was dragging his ass. But the point no longer had the urge or the energy to step up the pace and down him. Maybe he was putting on a show to keep the outfit intact? No, it was no show. He was in trouble and the slow, dragging steps were sending shocks of pain from his feet to his brain, almost paralyzing him with every step

'Highpockets is going to drop...Highpockets is going to drop... Highpockets is going to drop...'This became the cadence as we slugged step after miserable step. A singsong, silent chant was on every lip and every eye was on Sam Huxley, whose face was wrenched in pain. He clenched his teeth to fight off the blackness creeping over him. 'Huxley's folding...Huxley's folding...'A mile, another. We neared Otaki again. Our pace was almost nil. Five men keeled over in quick succession. We pulled to a halt.

We were finished and we knew it. We'd never make the last day. Fifty men were out now and the time was past for fighting climax after climax. The saturation point was past. No miracle had happened.

Sam Huxley felt nothing in his long legs. He pinched and rubbed for an hour to get feeling back. He looked at his watch like a nervous cat from where he sat propped against a tree. His only order was to get up the galley along the highway quickly. It didn't make sense to put it so close to the road.

What was he up to? Suddenly he sprang to his feet and shouted, 'Get your mess gear and line up along the road for chow, on the double!'

We staggered up the highway to where the field kitchen was. Eight hundred and fifty men, and the officers at the head of the line. Huxley kept looking at his watch every few seconds. Then he smiled as the sound of motors was heard coming over the Otaki Bridge. Huxley had passed his miracle!

Trucks rolled down near us. In them sat the men of Pawnee Blue, the Third Battalion was coming back from Foxton. On their asses!

'Candy-asssed Marines!' A roar went up from us on the roadside, 'Candy-assed Marines!' The red-faced men of the Third Battalion held their tongues, ashamed of their position.

'Candy - asses...candy-asses!'

'Say, what outfit is that?'

'Why that's the Third Battalion, cousin.'

'Worthless as tits on a bull!'

'Ain't they sweet!'

'Whatsamatter, candy - asses? Road too hard for you boys?'

'Maybe they're Doug's soldiers.'

The trucks roared out of sight. I felt wonderful. I felt like bursting inside. Huxley was standing on top of a table, his hands on his hips. 'Well,' he roared, 'shall I call the trucks up for us, or does the Second Battalion walk?'

'The hell with chow!' A cheer went up.

'And when we hit the camp gate,' Huxley shouted over the din, 'let's show them what the best outfit in the Corps looks like,' (Uris 494-502).

Stevie thought about dying in battle. Indeed he had spoken of it with Mike, his peer and colleague and friend. In a letter Mike wrote to his girlfriend, Elysee, he told what Stevie had said about dying, "that he would die a happy man." A complete man, as he had known Donna and married her and found happiness. In Battle Cry there is a brief mention of the preparations being made for battle:

"We reduced speed as another convoy equal to ours in size passed us. It was the Army division heading for Makin. Dry run or not, reserve or not, each man cleaned his weapon again, made peace with God, wrote his letter home and waited," (Uris 530).

SEMPER FIDELIS

In Flanders Field

by

Lt. Col. John McCrae

In Flanders Fields the poppies blow
Between the crosses,, row on row,
That mark our place, and in the sky
The larks, still bravely singing, fly
Scarce heard amid the guns below.

We are the Dead. Short days ago
We lived, felt dawn, saw sunset glow,
Loved and were loved, and now we lie
In Flanders fields.

Take up our quarrel with the foe;
To you from failing hands we throw
The torch; be yours to hold it high.
If ye break faith with us who die
We shall not sleep, though poppies grow
In Flanders fields.

The author of this poem, a member of the First Canadian Contingent, died in France on January 28, 1918, after four years of service on the Western Front.

Times Are A Changing

The Times He Lived In

Stevie was born July 14, 1943 and he died June 3, 1967. Both times were a time of war and in a letter to his son, Daddy wrote to Stevie upon his birth, that there would be another war coming. After World War II ended the Cold War started with its threats of Communism taking over the countries of the world. This threat permeated the politics and religion of the era Stevie lived in. It shaped the culture and the youth of the world. This singular threat created the pervasive idea of The Domino Theory in which it was felt, in Democratic policies, that if one country became communist then its' neighbors would also follow suit. This theory would result in the involvement of the United States of America in the Korean War and the Viet Nam War. The wars would create the stupor of the 50's and the uprising of the 60's. It would cost Steve his life in service to his country and his belief in The Domino Theory.

It was a time of Howdy Doody on the newly invented television, crew cuts, poodle skirts, saddle shoes, cowboy and Indians and, rhythm and blues, jazz, rock and roll and hi-fi's, along with the building of the bomb shelter and carports. The ranch house became the norm and suburbia started a new way of living with your neighbors, people left the cities for the countryside; the extended family was scattered and nursing homes took the place of family.

There were sweeping changes in government and federal services to the citizens of the United States. The New Deal was replaced with the Great Society and Medicare and Medicaid and Social Security were begun. An interstate highway system was started, taken from the German Autobahn, and it changed the way Americans traveled and worked and lived. The Civil Rights movement was started first with the desegregation of the Armed Forces and then desegregation of the schools and public places. There were five President's during Stevie's lifetime and three Popes. The Popes brought the Church into the 20th century and for the first time the Pope left the Vatican and became a pilgrim in his own right. The television and radio brought politics and religion right into the home and everyone became an expert on any number of topics.

Franklin Delano Roosevelt was the first president under which Steve lived. He was the 32nd President and he was a liberal Democrat. He was the only president to have served more than two terms in office, serving four - from 1933-1945. He came into office in a time of worldwide economic crisis and world war. To counter these times, he introduced the program called the New Deal: he introduced the Federal Deposit Insurance Corporation (FDIS), he introduced the Tennessee Valley Authority (TVA), he introduced the U.S. Securities and Exchange commission (SEC), he introduced the Social Security System and finally he introduced the National Labor Relations Board (NLRB). After 1943, FDR was involved with the Yalta Conference, which played a critical role in post-war world policies along with the creation of the United Nations. His New Deal Coalition dominated the Democratic Party until the late '60's. He and his wife, Eleanor, remain touchstones for modern American liberalism. President Roosevelt was ranked as one of America's greatest presidents.

The Cold War strategy was created in 1943 at the Cairo Conference where FDR met with Generalissimo Chiang Kai-Shek and Winston Churchill; Joseph Stalin was not present at that meeting. The Big-Three (The Allies in the fight to conquer Hitler.) were FDR, Churchill and Stalin with Chiang Kai-Shek cooperating informally on the Pacific Front. The Big Three concentrated in the West; Russian troops fought on the Eastern Front; Chinese, British, and American troops fought in the Pacific. In 1945 FDR spoke about the "Crimean Conference" which "ought to spell the end of a system of unilateral action, the exclusive Alliances, the spheres of influence, the balances of power, and all the other expedients that have been tried for centuries — and have always failed. We propose to substitute for all these a universal organization in which all peace loving nations will finally have a chance to join." Hence, the United Nations. In 1945 Stalin accused the other allies of making a secret pact with Hitler and the Schism was permanent. Roosevelt replied to this charge, "I cannot avoid a feeling of bitter resentment towards your informers, whoever they are, for such vile misrepresentations of my actions or those of my trusted subordinates."

On March 30, 1945, FDR traveled to Warm Springs, Georgia to rest before his anticipated appearance at the founding of the U.N. On the afternoon of April 12, 1945, FDR said, "I have a terrible headache" and was carried to his bedroom where he died of a cerebral hemorrhage. A close friend, Allen Drury, later said, "So ended an era, and so began another." Harry S. Truman, FDR's Vice-President, was sworn in as the 33rd president of the United States.

Harry S. Truman was born May 8, 1884, and died December 26, 1972; he was the 33rd president and served two terms as a Democrat. Though his in-office poll ratings were low he is ranked as one of America's greatest presidents. He succeeded President Franklin D. Roosevelt on April 12, 1945, when the President died of a brain hemorrhage. From that date until 1949, President Truman had no vice president but from 1949-1953 his Vice President was Alben Barkley. Truman served as Missouri's Senator from 1935-1945. He first gained national attention with his Truman Committee and replaced Harry A. Wallace as FDR's running mate in 1945. He won re-election in 1948 but had not been favored to win - his famous "Whistle Stop Tour" of rural America made him more famous and won him the election.

One of his first acts as president was to use his Executive Veto Power to desegregate the US Armed Forces. Truman's Presidency was eventful in foreign affairs, with the end of World War II and his decision to use nuclear weapons against Japan, the founding of the United Nations, the Marshall Plan to rebuild Europe, the Truman Doctrine to contain communism, the beginning of the cold War, the creation of the North Atlantic Treaty Organization and the Korean War. His term's as President were disturbed by waves of corruption within his Cabinet and senior White House staff. Republican's made corruption a central issue in the Eisenhower 1957 election campaign.

Truman was a folksy, unassuming president. He popularized such phrases as "the buck stops here", and "If you can't stand the heat, you better get out of the kitchen." Despite negative public opinion during his terms in office, popular and scholarly assessments of his presidency earned him the rating, upon his retirement, as one of America's greatest Presidents. Truman's legendary upset victory in 1948, over Thomas E. Dewey is routinely invoked by underdog presidential candidates His main interests were music (he played the piano), reading and history. He served as a captain in World War I after memorizing the eye screening chart for entrance into the armed forces as he had such bad eyesight. He married Bess Wallace in 1918 after proposing twice to her, once before the War and again after the War. He was the first president, after 1897, not to earn a college degree, again due to his poor eyesight. His war record made it possible for him to enter politics in Missouri and later, on the national stage.

The Truman Committee, which brought him to FDR's attention, was a committee which investigated the scandal of military wastefulness by exposing fraud and mismanagement. The Committee was a success and is reported to have saved the US government 15 billion dollars.

The Manhattan Project was the Project which authorized the use of atomic weapons against the Japanese in August 1945 after the failure of the Potsdam Declaration. On August 6, 1945, at 8:15AM, the B-29 bomber Enola Gay dropped an atomic bomb on Hiroshima. Two days later, having heard nothing from the Japanese government, a second Atomic Bomb was dropped on Nagasaki on August 9, 1945. The Japanese agreed to surrender on August 14, 1945. The President later said, "I knew what I was doing when I stopped the war...I have no regrets and, under the same circumstances, I would do it again."

Faced with Communist abandonment of commitments to democracy which were made at the Potsdam Conference and Communist advances into Greece and Turkey that suggested a hunger for global domination, the Cold War began and Truman concluded that the interests of the Soviet Union were quickly becoming incompatible with those of the U.S. The Truman Administration articulated an increasingly hard line against the Soviets. Truman won support for the Truman Doctrine, which formalized a policy of containment, and the Marshall Plan, which aimed to help rebuild Europe. As part of the U.S. Cold War strategy, Truman signed the National Security Act of 1947 and reorganized military forces by merging the Department of War and the Department of the Navy into the Department of Defense and created the United States Air Force. The Act also created the CIA and the National Security Council. He was also a major player in the establishment of the Jewish state in the Palestine Mandate. On January 7, 1953, President Truman announced the detonation of the first US hydrogen bomb. In 1952, Truman was a strong supporter of the creation of NATO (North Atlantic Treaty Organization) which established a formal peacetime military alliance with those nations that had not fallen into Soviet control. The US, the United Kingdom, France, Italy, The Netherlands, Belgium, Luxembourg, Norway, Denmark, Portugal, Iceland and Canada were the original treaty signatories.

Throughout his terms of office, Truman had to deal with accusations that the Federal Government was harboring Soviet spies at the highest level. McCarthyism was the result. Senator Joseph McCarthy quickly established himself as a national figure and his explosive allegations dominated the headlines. His claims were short on confirmable details, but they nevertheless transfixed a nation struggling to come to grips with frightening new realities: the Soviet Union's nuclear explosion, the loss of US atom bomb secrets, the fall of China to Communism and new revelations of Soviet intelligence penetration of other US agencies, including the Treasury Department. The Kennedy's supported Senator Joseph McCarthy and his intrusive and embittered battling with Americans as to whether they were communists or not. Many notables were blacklisted by the government.

June 25, 1950—the North Korean People's Army invaded South Korea, precipitating the outbreak of the Korean War. Stunned, the President called for a naval blockade of Korea and the UN intervened. The War lasted three years and ended up with the division of Korea into the North and South boundary of the 38th parallel. At the same time as the time of the Korean War the White House was gutted as it was deemed structurally unsafe and had to be rebuilt.

The White House was gutted, except for the newer West Wing and the Oval Office. The exterior was shored up and left intact and the new Truman Balcony was deemed structurally sound and was left alone. Truman lived across the street in the Blair House and had to walk across the street to get to work each day. On one of those days, November 1, 1950, Puerto Rican nationalists attempted to assassinate Truman as he crossed the street from Blair House to the Oval Office. One conspirator was shot dead, as was a Secret Service agent, and the other conspirator was wounded and sentenced to death but the President later commuted his sentence to life in prison. Following this attempt on the Truman's life the US ratified the 22nd Amendment making a president ineligible to be elected for a second time after having served more than two years of a previous presidential term.

In the time of electing a new president, Dwight David Eisenhower, a Republican, campaigned against what he denounced as Truman's failures regarding "Korea, Communism and Corruption." and the "Mess in Washington" and Eisenhower promised to go to Korea once more. He defeated Stevenson, the Democratic contender, ending 20 years of Democratic rule. While Truman and Eisenhower had previously been friends, Truman felt betrayed that Eisenhower did not denounce Joseph McCarthy during the campaign. Truman died of multiple organ failure due to pneumonia on December 26, 1972, but not before Lyndon Baines Johnson signed into law the Medicare Bill at the Truman Library and gave the first two cards to Truman and his wife, Bess to honor him for his fight for government health care while he was president.

Dwight David Eisenhower (Ike) was born on October 14, 1890 and died May 28, 1969. He was the 34th president and he was a Republican. He kept pressure on the Soviet Union during the Cold War and made nuclear weapons a higher priority, launched the space race, enlarged Social Security and began the interstate highway system. He is ranked as one of the greatest presidents. He graduated from West Point in 1915 and became a 5 star general during the course of World War II.

After Pearl Harbor, Ike was assigned to the General Staff in Washington, DC where he served until June of 1942, with responsibility for creating plans to defeat Japan and Germany. Later he was appointed to Assistant Chief of Staff in charge of Operations Division under Chief of Staff General George C. Marshall. It was this close association that formally brought Ike to senior command positions. Marshall recognized his great organizational and administration abilities. Ike never saw the front lines.

In January of 1944, he was officially designated the Supreme Allied Commander of the Allied Expeditionary Force. He received his 4th star. On December 20, 1944, he was promoted to General of the Army and received his 5th star.

In 1948, Ike became President of Columbia University and in December of 1950 he took leave when he became Supreme Commander of NATO. He retired from that position in 1952 and returned to Columbia. In 1952, a "Draft Eisenhower" movement in the Republican Party persuaded him to declare his candidacy in the 1952 presidential campaign. He won the nomination and ran against the Democrat Adlai Stevenson whom he handily defeated. Ike was the last president to be born in the 19th century and the oldest since James Buchanan in 1856 at the age of 62. He was the only general in the 20th century to serve as president.. Throughout his presidency he preached a doctrine of dynamic conservatism. He continued all the major New Deal programs still in operation, especially Social Security and made the agency a new Cabinet level position under the name Department of Health, Education and Welfare. One of Ike's most enduring achievements was championing and signing the bill that authorized the Interstate Highway System of 1956. He thought an Interstate Highway System would not only be beneficial for military operations but be the building block for continued economic growth.

After the Suez Crisis in 1958, the U.S. became the protector of most Western interests in the Middle East. Ike proclaimed the "Eisenhower Doctrine" in January of 1957, stating that in relation to the Middle East, the US would be "prepared to use armed force...to counter aggression from any country controlled by international communism". Eisenhower explored the option of supporting the French colonial forces in Vietnam who were Fighting an independence insurrection there. However, Chief of Staff Matthew Ridgeway, dissuaded the President from intervening by presenting a comprehensive estimate of the massive military deployment that would be necessary. Stevie was Killed in Action in Vietnam nine years later.

President Eisenhower supported the 1954 "Brown v Board of Education of Topeka" US Supreme court decision in which segregated schools were ruled to be unconstitutional. He proposed the Civil Rights Act of 1957 and 1960 and signed those Acts into law; those Acts constituted the first significant civil rights acts since the 1870s. The "Little Rock Nine" incident of 1957 happened at this time with Arkansas refusing to obey a federal court order to integrate their schools. The National Guard was called in to Little Rock to quell an uprising of whites. Other notable events happened during this time: Alaska became the 49th state on January 3, 1959, and Hawaii became the 50th state on August 21, 1959.

Ike was the first post-president to come under the protection of the Former Presidents Act. Under the Act Ike was entitled to receive a lifetime pension, state provided staff, and a Secret Service detail. That Act has now been modified to Secret Service detail for ten years post presidency. Eisenhower, who was the oldest elected president in history at that time, handed over power to the youngest elected president - President John Fitzgerald Kennedy, who defeated Richard Nixon by a narrow margin.

On March 28, 1969, President Dwight David Eisenhower died of congestive heart failure and is buried on the grounds of the Eisenhower Presidential Library in Aibelene, Kansas.

John Fitzgerald Kennedy was elected the 35th President of the United States on January 20, 1961 and he served until November 22, 1963 when he was assassinated. He was born May 29, 1917, and died on that fateful day of November 22, 1963: he was 46 years old. He was known by the nickname "Jack." He married Jacqueline Lee Bouvier Kennedy in a Roman Catholic ceremony on September 12, 1953, and he was the first Roman Catholic president. He was also the youngest president being just 43 years old. He was born in Brookline, Massachusetts. He graduated from Harvard with a degree in International Affairs in June of 1940. His senior thesis was published under the title "Why England Slept." He is the only president to have received the Pulitzer Prize for his book "*Profiles In Courage*," published in 1957. During World War II, he served as Commander of the Motor Torpedo Boat PT-109 in the Pacific. His adventures during this period have been chronicled in movies and books and the sinking of his ship resulted in his chronic back problems.

Before entering politics he thought he would be a journalist, but after his brother's death in World War II he ran for office in Boston and became a Congressman from Massachusetts, serving for six years. On January 2, 1960, JFK officially declared his intent to run for president. At the Democratic Convention he delivered his famous "New Frontier" speech, which represented the changes America and the rest of the world would be going through. On July 13, 1960 the Democratic Convention nominated JFK as its candidate for president. He chose Lyndon Baines Johnson as his running mate as he needed the strength of LBJ in the South to win what was considered the closest race since 1916.

The major issues at that time in America's history were getting the economy moving again, Kennedy's Roman Catholicism, Cuba, and whether the Soviet space and missile programs had surpassed those of the US. In September and October of 1960, Kennedy and Nixon debated on the first televised presidential debate in US history. The debates are now considered a milestone in American political history — the point at which the medium of TV began to play a dominate role in national politics.

On April 17, 1961, Kennedy enacted an Eisenhower decision to invade Cuba. It was called the "Bay of Pigs Invasion" and was led by 1,500 US trained Cuban exiles. Kennedy, however, did not order naval or air support and the invaders were killed or captured by Castro's army. Kennedy was forced to negotiate the release of 1,189 survivors. After 20 months, Cuba released the captives in exchange for 53 million dollars worth of food and medicine. Castro feared further invasions by the US and on October 16, 1962, Kennedy was shown photos of a Soviet intermediate-range ballistic missile site under construction in Cuba. The President ordered a naval quarantine of Cuban waters inspecting all ships arriving in Cuba. To avoid nuclear war,

Kennedy and Khrushchev reached an agreement that stated that the Soviet Union would remove the missiles subject to UN inspections if the US publicly promised never to invade Cuba and quietly removed the missiles stationed in Turkey. The crisis was over but Cuba remains Communist to this day.

As one of the President's first acts as the newly elected leader of the Free World, Kennedy asked Congress to create the Peace Corps and through this program American volunteers would help underdeveloped nations in areas such as education, farming, health care, and construction. Also, Vista was created which enabled the same type of volunteerism to poverty prone areas of the US. Both programs are still strong within the American political system.

With the release of the "The Pentagon Papers" in 1971, the American public came to know of Kennedy's involvement with Vietnam. Proclaiming a fight against Communism, Kennedy enacted policies providing political, economic, and military support for the unstable French installed South Vietnamese government. This included sending 16,000 Special Forces fighting men who were "advisors." Kennedy also agreed to free-fire zones, napalm, defoliants, and jet planes. US involvement in the area continually escalated until regular US forces were directly fighting the Vietnam War in the next administration. Had he lived, things may have proved differently as Kennedy had plans to withdraw troops after the 1964 election.

June 26, 1963, saw Kennedy give his famous "Freedom" speech in which he says,"Ich bin ein Berliner." Nearly 5/6s of Berliners were on the square that day and the speech had to do with a divided Germany and the Berlin Wall. The speech criticized Communism. In August of 1963, Kennedy signed into law the Partial Test Ban Treaty which prohibited atomic testing on the ground, in the atmosphere or underwater. The United States, the United Kingdom, and the Soviet Union were the original signatories.

Kennedy called his domestic program the "New Frontier." It provided for promised federal funding for education, medical care for the elderly, and government intervention to halt the recession. Kennedy also promised an end to racial discrimination in 1963. On June 11, 1963, after many racial civil rights interventions, Kennedy made his famous civil rights address on national television; this was the final result of white southerners blocking blacks from public schools. He proposed a tax reform which included income tax cuts. Few of Kennedy's major programs passed Congress during his lifetime, although under Johnson they became law in 1964-65. On July 20,

1969, almost six years after JFK's death and desire to lead the space race, Project Apollo was finally realized when men landed on the moon.

The First Family was very popular influencing fashion trends and becoming the focus in innumerable photo shoots and magazines and newspaper articles. They were like pop stars. On May 19, 1962, Marilyn Monroe sang her famous "Happy Birthday Mr. President" song in her equally famous evening gown at Madison Square Garden to a sold out crowd of well wishers. The charisma of the Kennedy's led to the figurative designation of "Camelot" for his administration.

In October, 1951, during his 3rd term as Congressman, he invited eight year younger brother Bobby and his sister, Patricia, on an eight week long Asian trip. For the first time, John F. Kennedy drew close to his younger brother, who had just graduated from law school and when he became President he named his brother, Bobby, to be his Cabinet level position of Attorney General. Bobby was later assassinated on June 6, 1968, during his first run for President.

President John F. Kennedy was assassinated in Dallas, Texas, at 12:30PM EST on November 22, 1963. He was shot twice in the neck and head by Lee Harvey Oswald. Oswald was captured that same day in a movie theater and claimed he was innocent. He was jailed and on being transported to a hearing two days later he was in turn shot and killed by Jack Ruby. Lyndon Johnson instituted the Warren Commission to investigate the assassination of JFK and the Commission concluded that Oswald was the assassin with the probability of conspiracy. The event had great impact on US history because of its impact on the nation and the ensuing political repercussions. President Kennedy is buried at Arlington Cemetery with an eternal flame burning together with his wife and minor children. The burial was held March 14, 1963. Steve is buried very close by.

Kennedy's continuation of President Truman's and President Eisenhower's policies of giving economic and military aid to the Vietnam War preceded by Johnson's escalation of the conflict resulted in 550,000 US fighting men and women giving aid to the Vietnamese. This contributed to a decade of national difficulties and disappointment on the political and social-minded landscape.

Lyndon Baines Johnson was sworn in as the 36th President immediately upon the death of John F. Kennedy in Air Force One by a woman judge with his hand on a Catholic missal. His wife, Lady Bird, and Jacqueline Kennedy were there. He was a Democrat and completed JFK's term and then ran for his own term. He served from 1963-1969. LBJ was a major player in the Democratic Party and as president was responsible for designing the "Great Society" legislation that included civil rights laws, Medicare and Medicaid, aid to education and the "War on Poverty." Simultaneously, he escalated the American involvement in the Vietnam War from 16,000 in 1963 to 500,000 in 1968. Johnson's popularity as president steadily declined after the 1966 Congressional elections and his reelection bid in the 1968 campaign. His reelection collapsed as a result of turmoil within the Democratic Party and the country related to the Vietnam War. There was warfare in Vietnam and warfare within America; this was to be found on the college campuses and the inner cities.

LBJ married Lady Bird in Texas on November 17, 1934. The following year he entered politics, serving in the House from 1937-1949. He received a Silver Star in World War II for his role in the Pacific participating as an observer on board a combat bomber. He was assigned to MacArthur through President Roosevelt. Johnson's mission had a substantial impact because it led to upgrading the South Pacific Theater and aided the overall war effort immensely. Following the war, Johnson was elected to the Senate in 1948 in a controversial and "rigged" election. He won by 87 votes, but his election was dubbed "Landslide Johnson" which he often used deprecatingly to refer to himself. In 1951, Johnson was chosen Senate Majority Whip and served until 1953. In the 1952 general election, the Democrats lost to the Republicans and Johnson became the Senate Minority Whip. In the 1954 election the Democrats won and the Republicans lost and LBJ became the Senate Majority Whip. Working with Eisenhower and Sam Rayburn, he was responsible for the passage of the Civil Rights Act of 1957, the first civil rights legislation passed by the Senate since the American Revolution. In conjunction with the civil rights movement, Johnson overcame Southern resistance and convinced Congress to pass the Civil Rights Act of 1964, which outlawed most forms of racial segregation. In 1967, he nominated civil rights attorney Thurgood Marshall to be the first African-American Associate Justice of the Supreme Court.

On September 7, 1964, Johnson's election campaign ran the famous "The Daisy Ad" which played depicting a little girl picking petals from a daisy, counting up to ten. Then a baritone voice took over, counted down from ten to zero and a nuclear bomb exploded, indicating that rival Barry Goldwater meant nuclear war. The ad was removed after only a few days but it remains famous and helped put LBJ in the White House. It was the largest landslide victory in the history of Presidential elections.

Then came 1965 and the loss of American innocence.

1965 started as a year of uplifted society and liberal programs. It ended with the greatest escalation of troops to Vietnam seen to that point and riots in Watts and Washington, DC and other areas where there were large concentrations of African-Americans living in poor conditions. There were huge anti-war demonstrations in major cities and two men set themselves on fire and died in protest to America's growing involvement in Vietnam.

President Johnson's Great Society, which started out so glowingly and positive and liberal, ended with a current of growing conservatism and upswing in the Republican Party. What had started out as cohesiveness in the country ended in dissipation and the birth of the culture of "The Sixties": Draft cards were being burned publicly, and bras were being burned as women became to think of men as their oppressors.

In mid 1965, Johnson ordered 50,000 more men to Vietnam and doubled the draft. The political scene was being transformed just as the cultural scene was being transformed – neither one in harmony with the other.

And this is the climate that prevailed as Stevie graduated from Princeton University. No wonder his searching and then resolve. He knew in his heart that Communism must be stopped in its tracks and that keeping South Vietnam a democracy was the right thing to fight for. Others would disagree, but Stevie was not alone.

The "Great Society" program, with its name coined from one of Johnson's speeches, became LBJ's agenda for Congress in January, 1965: aid to education, attack on disease, Medicare, urban renewal, beautification, conservation, development of depressed regions, a wider scale fight against poverty, control and prevention of crime, and removal of the obstacles to the right to vote. Congress enacted many of these proposals. But the "Great Society" was in trouble; urban riots in major black ghettos caused a series of "long hot summers." It started in Harlem in 1964 and then in the Watts District of Los Angeles in 1965 and extended through to the summers of 1970. The biggest wave came in 1968 in the wake of the assassination of Dr.

Martin Luther King, Jr. Newark burned in 1967, where six days of rioting left 26 dead, 1,500 wounded and the inner city a burned out shell. In Detroit, in 1967, 7400 National Guard troops were sent to quell fire bombs and the like. Johnson finally sent in tanks, machine guns and tear gas. Forty-three were dead 2,250 injured, 4,000 arrested, property damage in the hundreds of millions. Detroit's inner city was never rebuilt. LBJ called for billions to be spent in the cities and another civil rights law regarding housing to be enacted, but his political career was tarnished and the "Great Society" programs lost support.

Johnson's problems began to mount in 1966. The press sensed a "credibility gap" between what Johnson was saying in press conferences and what was happening on the ground in Vietnam, this led to much less favorable coverage of LBJ. He firmly believed in the "Domino Theory" and that his containment policy required America to make a serious effort to stop all Communist aggression. LBJ jumped the numbers of fighting men and women from 16,000 to 550,000 during his terms in office, especially after the Gulf of Tonkin Incident in 1964. The Gulf of Tonkin Resolution, which gave the president the exclusive right to use military force without consulting the Senate, was based on a false pretext, as he later admitted. It was LBJ who began America's direct involvement in the ground war in Vietnam. By 1968, over 550,000 American soldiers were inside Vietnam; in 1967 and 1968 they were being killed at the rate of over 1,000 each month, and Stevie was one of them. LBJ often privately cursed the war and said he "was trying to win it just as fast as I can in every way that I know how."

After leaving the presidency in 1969, LBJ went home to his ranch in Johnson City, Texas. In his will he donated the ranch to the public to form the LBJ National Historical Park with the provision that the ranch "remain a working ranch and not become a sterile relic of the past." Johnson died of a 3rd heart attack on January 22, 1973. Johnson was buried at the family cemetery near his birthplace in Stonewall, Texas.

As Stevie was Roman Catholic he grew up under the care of three Popes of Rome: Pope Pius XI, Pope John XXIII, and Pope Paul VI. These three Popes, more than any others up to that time brought the church into the 20th century and for the first time the popes left the safety of the Vatican to become pilgrims of the world.

Pope Pius XII reigned from March 2, 1939, until his death on October 9, 1958. He was 82 when he died and was one of the longest serving popes. Pope Pius XII explained the Catholic faith in 41 encyclicals and almost 1,000 messages during his reign. He served as Pope during the Holocaust and was a lone voice in Europe in support of the Jews and is considered a "Righteous Gentile" by the members of the Jewish faith. He required bishops throughout the church to initiate biblical studies to lay people, something that had not been done previously as the church felt lay persons reading the *Bible* would interpret it wrong or not understand its meanings.

On the very day (May 3, 1917) Our Lady of Fatima appeared Pope Pius XII was consecrated a bishop and he remained a staunch supporter and believer of the doctrine of the Blessed Virgin Mary. He consecrated the world to the Immaculate Heart of Mary in 1942, in accordance with the second secret of Our Lady of Fatima. The dogma of the bodily assumption of the Virgin Mary is the crowning of the theology of Pope Pius XII. He was, also, the first to determine that the use of pain medication in terminally ill patients is justified, even if it means shortening that life. He was the first pope to accept the rhythm method of birth control as valid and good and a moral form of family planning. To Pius XII science and religion were heavenly sisters who could not possibly contradict each other over the long term. In 1950, Pope Pius XII acknowledged that evolution might accurately describe the biological origins of human life, but criticized those who use it as a religion. Fifty years later, Pope Paul II upheld the decision of Pius XII regarding the human soul: "Even if the human body originates from per-existent living matter, the spiritual soul is spontaneously created by God."

Pope Pius XII died on October 9, 1958, of acute heart failure; his cause of canonization was opened on November 18, 1965, by Pope Paul II. In March, 2007 the congregation recommended that Pius XII should be declared "venerable."

Pope John XXIII was elected to succeed Pius XII. He reigned from October 9, 1958, until his death on June 3,1963. He was the 261st pope. Upon his election he chose the name John as his regnal name. This was the first time in over 500 years that the name had been chosen - previous popes had avoided using this name as the last man to use this name came to be considered an Antipope —following the Western Schism in the 14th and 15th centuries that ended in 1417 with the election of an undisputed pope.

Pope John XXIII's personal warmth, good humor and kindness captured the world's affections in a way his predecessor, Pius XII, for all his great learning and personal holiness, had failed to do. On December 25, 1958, he became the first Pope to leave Vatican territory since 1870; he visited children suffering from polio at the Bambin Gesu Hospital and then visited Santo Spirito Hospital. The next day he visited Rome's Regina Coeli prison where he told the prisoners, "You could not come to me, so I came to you." Upon his death he was elected to the level of "Blessed" and was beatified.

He called for the Second Vatican Council but did not live to see it completed. From the Second Vatican Council came changes that reshaped the face of Catholicism: a comprehensive revised theology, a stronger emphasis on ecumenism, and a new approach to the world.

On September 23, 1962, Pope John XXIII was diagnosed with gastric carcinoma, but the news was kept from the public. On May 11, 1963, he made his last public appearance by accepting the Italian award, the Balzan Prize, for his engagement for peace. He died June 3, 1963. Lyndon Baines Johnson awarded him the Presidential Medal of Freedom.

Pope Paul VI succeeded John XXIII on June 3, 1963, and reigned until his death on August 6, 1978. Pope Paul VI was a Marian Pope and named Mary to be the Mother of the Church during the Vatican Council, which he completed after the death of predecessor.

Pope Paul VI sought dialog with the world, with other Christians, religions, atheism, excluding no one. He saw himself as an humble servant for a suffering humanity and demanded significant changes of the rich in America and Europe in favor of the poor in the Third World. His pontificate took place during sometimes revolutionary changes in the world; student revolts, the Vietnam War, and other upheavals. Paul VI tried to understand it all but at the same time defend the "Deposit of Faith" as it was entrusted to him. He was nicknamed the "Pilgrim Pope" as he visited six continents including a trip to the U.S.A. where, in front of the UN, he pleaded for peace for Vietnam. Pope Paul VI visited the Orthodox Patriarchs of Jerusalem and Constantinople in 1964 and 1967 . He was the first pope since the 9th century to visit the East, labeling the Eastern Churches as sister churches. Paul VI was the first pope to receive the Anglican Archbishop of Canterbury in official audience as "Head of the Church"; this was the first acknowledgment of the Church of England since King Henry XVIII.

On August 6, 1978, he died of a massive myocardial infarction. The diocesan process for beatification of "Servant of God Paul VI" began on May 11, 1993, by Pope John Paul II.

Stevie was very aware of the culture and times he lived in. He was not naive but was very wise to the ways of the world and what the coming trends would be. He was a Republican and very strait-laced; his manners and mannerisms were impeccable. He showed me music and styles of dress. He shared his morality with me. He was very family - centered and shared all his loves with all. Despite his long absence at private school he was always close by and ready to lend a helping hand. Pop culture influenced him but did not alter his basic goodness and decency. Music was a great love of his as he played and listened to it as much as he could. He never entered the culture that was "The Sixties."

He was born into the era of the Big Bands: bands like Glenn Miller and Duke Ellington, Louis Armstrong and Ella Fitzgerald but his awakening came with Bill Haley and the Comets in 1952. Bill Haley was one the world's first rock n' roll musicians. He was born on July 6, 1925, and died on February 9, 1981, seeing for himself the changes he wrought. He is credited with first popularizing this form of new music in the mid '50's with his group Bill Haley and the Comets. They burst upon the air waves with their first hit "Rock Around the Clock' and it changed music forever. "Shake, Rattle 'n Roll" was one of the first ever rock 'n roll songs to hit the British charts and sold over a million copies and influenced the young Paul McCartney and John Lennon. Bill Haley is known as the "Father of Rock 'N Roll."

Another rocker was Fats Domino, and he influenced Steve's music and playing abilities. Fats was born on February 26, 1928, and is still living. He attracted national attention with his record from 1949, "The Fat Man." This recording, which sold over a million copies, is considered the first rock 'n roll record to do so. Fats Domino recorded over 60 singles from 1949-1962 for Imperial Records, placing 40 songs in the top 10 on the rhythm and blues charts and scoring 11 top 10 singles on the pop charts. By the end of 1964 the British Invasion had changed the tastes of the record buying public. The Beatles recorded Domino's songs. In 1965 the Rolling Stones introduced their groundbreaking recording of "I Can't Get No Satisfaction." This song and the Stones shaped culture and young people in a way that had not happened since the World War II Big Bands and Glenn Miller. The song was a far cry from "How Much Is That Doggy In The Window" talking about sexuality and sensuousness in a manner that had never been done before and gotten away with. Movies changed also as teenagers flocked to theaters to see the Beatle's *Help* and *How To Stuff a Wild Bikini.* TV introduced the first African-American star to appear in a show: *I Spy* with Bill Cosby.

Stevie had the wonderful opportunity to play guitar with Bo Diddley, another pioneer of rock 'n roll. Bo Diddley was born December 30, 1928 and died on June 2, 2008. He was an influential and original American rock 'n roll singer, guitarist and songwriter. He was known as the "Originator" because of his key role in the transition from blues to rock 'n roll, influencing a host of legendary acts including Buddy Holly, Jimi Hendrix, and Eric Clapton among other luminaries. He introduced more insistent, driving rhythms and hard-edge guitar sound on a wide-moving catalog of songs: "Who Do You Love" and "Hey, Bo Diddley" are two of his more popular songs. In 1963, he starred in a UK concert tour with the Everly Brothers, Little Richard, and the then unknown Rolling Stones.

In 1963 Stevie introduced me to Joan Baez; he was a great fan of hers. She was a folksinger and songwriter and many of her songs deal with social issues. Her first album came out in 1959 after appearing at the Newport Folk Festival. Baez emerged at the forefront of the American roots revival where she introduced her audiences to as yet unknown Bob Dylan and was emulated by such artists as Emmylou Harris, Judy Collins, Joni Mitchell, and Bonnie Raitt. She was born on December 30, 1928 and is still living and recording.

Bob Dylan was another who shaped Stevie's musical life. Bob Dylan has gone through many metamorphoses, but when he was starting out he was pure folk and a chronicler of the times. He was born on May 24, 1941, and is still living. He is a singer, songwriter, author and poet who has been a major figure in popular music for five decades. The most celebrated works date from the early 60's when he became an influential story teller and a reluctant figurehead for America's unrest. "Blowing In The Wind" and "The Times They Are A 'Changing" became anthems of the Civil Rights movement.

The Beach Boys impressed Stevie quite a bit. They were an American rock band and were formed in 1961. The group gained popularity for its close vocal harmonies and lyrics reflecting a California youth culture of cars and surfing. Surfing was Stevie's passion. Lead Brian Wilson's growing creative ambitions later transformed them into a more artistically innovative group that earned critical praise and influenced many later musicians.

Stevie also introduced me to classical music as he brought to me Vivaldi's Trumpet Concerto and I fell in love with Baroque music and still, to this day, it is my favorite. Stevie dressed in the New England style which was called "preppy" and consisted of oxford button down shirts, bow ties and tweed jackets and chino slacks. He wore his curly hair on the short side but when he returned from his summer in Europe in 1965 his hair was the longest I had ever seen and he looked handsome. He was wearing a glen plaid summer suit, a pink shirt, and a bow tie and he had just come from his Foreign Service oral exam. He could have been a model for the department store, Brook Brothers. He ignored the dress styles of the 60's which included bell bottom jeans and flowered shirts and flowing hair. He ignored the cultural revolution except for what pleased him, mostly the music.

He knew his time had come when he heard Lyndon Baines Johnson's Selective Service speech in July of '65. He chose the honorable path and joined the Reserves; he had a great deal of honor.

EPILOGUE

A Wall Remembrance

Dear Stevie,

You are missed by many and loved by even more. I have been in touch with some of your fellow Marines who fought so bravely in Union II. They tell me you led by example and were a "gung ho young Marine officer who was well liked by his men." I am so proud of you.

Today, Eleanor, your new grand-niece, was born, June 2, 2009. A miracle on such a tragic day.

Love,
Mari
June 2, 2009

PEACETREES VIETNAM

PeaceTrees Vietnam, a nongovernmental organization based in Bainbridge Island, Washington, has been helping to strengthen ties between the United States and Vietnam by removing landmines, providing mine survivors benefits, teaching, mine-risk education, and planting trees in Vietnam for over a decade. The PeaceTrees Village Kindergarten was built and dedicated in memory of Dave Hackett and Steve Kelsey, US Marine Corps veterans who served in Quang Tri Province. Classmates from their Princeton class of '65 funded the school in their honor. The dedication plaque is located just inside the front door of the kindergarten and reads:

Funding for the construction of this school came from
friends, Princeton classmates and family of
Steve Kelsey and Dave Hackett
Dedicated in their memory on September 19, 2002
PeaceTrees Friendship Village Dong Ha Quang Tri province

PeaceTrees has to date accomplished the following incredible achievements: 400+ acres of land cleared; 27,659+ ordnance items removed; 40,000+ trees planted; 416 participants on 29 citizen diplomacy trips; mine awareness education provided for 14,000+ children; 100 family homes, 9 libraries and 4 kindergartens built; assistance to 640+ UXO victims and their families.

PeaceTrees Vietnam was founded in 1995 to renew relationships with the people of Vietnam and promote a safe, healthy future for its children. The work focuses on Quang Tri Province, an area heavily impacted by the legacy of war. Over the last 30 years, nearly 6,800 people in the province have been killed or maimed by landmines and unexploded ordnance. In one of every five cases the victim is a child. PeaceTrees Vietnam was founded by Jerilyn Brusseau, the sister of 1st Lieutenant Daniel B. Cheney, a U.S. Army helicopter pilot killed in action in 1969.

Staff Sergeant Louis "Rick" Barnes

Dear Rick,

It has been a wonderful experience to have corresponded with you and to get to know you and my brother better. I thank you so much for the time and effort you invested in the Commendation process.

Senator John Kerry sent the notarized testimonies to the Department of the Navy and the United States Marine Corps two weeks ago and the request was dismissed out of hand. The SILVER STAR will not be awarded to my brother.

Sadly and Sincerely,
Marianne Kelsey Orestis   October 25, 2012

Dear Marianne,

I'm sorry but you and I know of his actions. Maybe that is whats most important. Your brother has been in my thoughts since his loss. His brothers, that were with him know of his efforts for God and Country. We are all better people because of him. I will miss him til my last day on this earth. He is waiting for us all at the Gate.

Forever in his thoughts, Rick

Louis "Rick" Barnes   October 25, 2012

Dear Marianne,

I wrote this with tears in my eyes. I cry not for myself but for those great men that never had the chance to live a long happy life with their mothers and fathers and brothers and sisters and wives and children. I cry for the loss of such good friends and guys that could have brought so much more good to this world.

I leave you with my prayers, and knowing that I once knew a great man, your brother.

Semper Fi
Staff Sergeant Louis "Rick" Barnes

2nd Lt Straughan Downing Kelsey, Jr
Killed In Action June 3, 1967
21E – 47

"TAPS"

Day is Done

Gone the Sun,

From the lakes, from the hills, from the sky.

All is well,

Safety rest,

God is night

Bibliography

Brown, David B. and Tiffany Brown Holmes. *Battlelines. I*universe, 2005

Margolis, John. *The Last Innocent Year: America In 1964. The Beginning of the "Sixties."* New York: William Morrow And Company, Inc., 1999.

Marrin, Albert. *America And Vietnam: The Elephant And The Tiger.* Beautiful Feet Books, 2002.

Uris, Leon. *Battle Cry.* New York: Avon Books, 2005.